Serial Bibliographies for Medieval Studies

Published under the auspices of the
CENTER FOR MEDIEVAL AND RENAISSANCE STUDIES
University of California, Los Angeles

Publications of the
CENTER FOR MEDIEVAL AND RENAISSANCE STUDIES

1. Dissent and Reform in the Early Middle Ages
2. Leonardo's Legacy
3. Serial Bibliographies for Medieval Studies

Serial Bibliographies for Medieval Studies

Richard H. Rouse

assisted by

J. H. Claxton *and* M. D. Metzger

Berkeley and Los Angeles
UNIVERSITY OF CALIFORNIA PRESS
1969

University of California Press
Berkeley and Los Angeles, California
University of California Press, Ltd.
London, England
Copyright © 1969 by The Regents of the University of California
Library of Congress Catalog Card Number: 68:31637
Designed by W. H. Snyder
Printed in the United States of America

Contents

Introduction

The general expansion of medieval studies in recent decades places at the disposal of the medievalist, whatever his special interest may be, a rich array of material, provided he can avail himself of it. The major obstacle is the problem of threading his way through the increasingly complex maze of publications to find the items of value to him. Like the sciences, medieval studies suffer less from the lack, than from the inaccessibility, of information. Admittedly, it has long been difficult to keep abreast of new research even in one's own area of specialization; it is, obviously, a physical impossibility to have the same sort of awareness of all published work in the various disciplines which comprise or contribute to medieval studies. The medievalist is thus dependent upon bibliographies to gather, organize, and present these materials to him in the most meaningful fashion.

There is no serial bibliography that provides the comprehensive coverage of medieval studies which, for example, *L'année philologique* provides for classical studies. Instead, current research and publication in medieval studies are reported by a wealth of specialized bibliographies, the number of which increases yearly. However, there are two general impediments to their effectiveness. First, in spite of their number and value to medieval studies, these bibliographies are not as well known as they might be. Only a handful of those listed in the present work appear in Coulter and Gerstenfeld's *Historical Bibliographies,* or in the American Historical Association's *Guide to Historical Literature.*[1] The serial bibliographies which are included in the various introductions to historical study are often not distinguished from the monographic bibliographies, and hence their significance is obscured. The result is that graduate students are frequently unaware of what bibliographies exist, and many professional medievalists are familiar only with the bibliographies

[1] E. M. Coulter and M. Gerstenfeld, eds., *Historical Bibliographies: A Systematic and Annotated Guide* (Berkeley, 1935); and American Historical Association, *Guide to Historical Literature* (New York, 1961).

which survey their specific fields of interest. Second, there is a lack of coordination among the individual bibliographies themselves. As a result some areas, such as art and archaeology, intellectual and ecclesiastical history, are well reported by a number of excellent bibliographies — each, however, in part duplicating the others.[2] By comparison, such important fields as the history of England and of the Baltic Sea area, medieval Latin literature, economic history, and the history of technology are at present inadequately reported. Since medievalists cannot be expected to have firsthand knowledge of the profusion of existing bibliographies, and since work toward improving bibliographic coordination and control is dependent upon an accurate appraisal of the available resources, we felt that an annotated guide to these serial bibliographies would serve a useful purpose.

For a guide to serial bibliographies scholars have hitherto normally depended upon one of the four editions of *Index bibliographicus* begun by Godet and Vorstius in 1931.[3] This standard work was joined in 1958 by an annotated guide to serial bibliographies produced wholly or in part by French scholars, *Les bibliographies internationales specialisées courantes françaises ou à participation française,*[4] and in 1963 by a comprehensive short title list of serial bibliographies, the *Verzeichnis laufend erscheinender Bibliographien.*[5] These works, of course, are not constructed specifically for the subject specialist. Their scope and sweep are broad, items of interest are occasionally omitted, and their annotations are only of the most cryptic sort. The need for more detailed guides to the bibliographies of special areas has been recognized in several fields. In modern language studies a preliminary annotated guide to serial bibliographies was

[2] Duplication among the modern language bibliographies was discussed at some length by J. H. Fisher, "Serial Bibliographies in the Modern Languages and Literatures," *PMLA*, 66 (1951), 138–156.

[3] M. Godet and J. Vorstius, eds., *Index bibliographicus* (Berlin, 1931). The fourth edition, published by the Fédération internationale de documentation, was begun in 1959.

[4] Direction des bibliothèques de France, *Les bibliographies internationales specialisées courantes françaises ou à participation française* (Paris, 1958).

[5] Deutsche Forschungsgemeinschaft, *Verzeichnis laufend erscheinender Bibliographien* (Wiesbaden, 1963).

published by John Fisher in 1951.[6] A brief but interesting survey of the serial bibliographies in history was published by E. Zimmermann in 1955.[7] Eric Boehm recently published an annotated guide to serial bibliographies in the field of international relations, with the aid of a computer.[8] Serial bibliographies pertinent to Latin American studies were recently surveyed by F. Peraza Sarausa.[9] In the area of medieval studies, serial bibliographies and problems of bibliographic control have been the subject of a series of conferences organized by J. J. Murphy and R. J. Schoeck. Included in the report on the first of these, published by H. B. Gardner, C.S.B., is a short title list of serials which serve to inform the medievalist of recent publications.[10]

The purpose of the present work is to provide an introduction to the serial bibliographies which pertain wholly or in part to medieval studies. The following definitions and general principles, applied with some flexibility, have guided its compilation. By "serial" we mean those bibliographies which are current rather than retrospective, which are thus published in serial rather than monographic form, either as independent titles or as integral parts of other serials.[11] By "bibliographies" we mean those reports of published work which are the result of a conscious effort to gather, organize and present bibliographic information. Besides the conventional classified lists of publications we have thus included bibliographic essays, collections of select tables of contents of recent periodicals, and accessions lists of special

---

[6] Fisher, *op. cit.*

[7] E. Zimmermann, "Die laufenden Bibliographien der Geschichtswissenschaft," *Zeitschrift für Bibliothekswesen und Bibliographie*, 2 (1955), 198–213.

[8] E. H. Boehm, ed., *Bibliographies on International Relations and World Affairs: An Annotated Directory*, Bibliography and Reference Series, 2 (Santa Barbara, 1965).

[9] F. Peraza Sarausa, ed., *Bibliografías corrientes de la América latina*, Biblioteca del bibliotecario, 65 (Gainesville, 1966).

[10] H. B. Gardner, C.S.B., "Current Trends in Mediaeval Bibliography," *Mediaeval Studies*, 27 (1965), 309–321. Conferences held April 10–11, 1965, Providence; April 6–7, 1967, Toronto.

[11] We have included certain bibliographies which are not strictly speaking serially published, but which, nevertheless, at intervals do produce excellent guides to recently published work in their respective fields. Among these are *Répertoire international des médiévistes* (16); A. T. Milne, ed., *Writings on British History* (36); and J. D. Pearson, ed., *Index Islamicus* (98).

libraries.[12] These items perform one or both of two basic services: Some, because of their breadth of coverage, organization, and indexes, are meant to be searched, and their function is to provide a nearly definitive record of the meaningful publications in a given field. Others are meant to be read, and their basic purpose is to keep their readers abreast of recent publications in a given field. The distinguishing factor common to bibliographies of both types is that they result from a conscious and deliberate search for material. Conversely, on the basis of the same criterion we have excluded collections of book reviews and lists of books received (both originate with publishers rather than with bibliographers), the briefer collections of tables of contents of journals, the numerous *chroniques* of societies, reports of congresses and meetings, and necrologies. While these lists of activities and publications serve to keep their readers informed, they are not, generally speaking, the product of a search to gather and present bibliographic information. We have also excluded national bibliographies, the standard indexes to periodical literature, and serial guides to dissertations. These bibliographies are adequately described in the standard guides to reference materials.

The scope of "medieval studies" has been broadly interpreted. Chronologically, the Middle Ages are considered to encompass the centuries which fall between the emergence of Christianity and the voyages of exploration. Thus, we have included certain bibliographies whose main emphasis is on classical or renaissance studies, but which nevertheless contain material of significant interest to the medievalist, such as *L'année philologique* **(251)** and the *Bibliographie internationale de l'humanisme et de la Renaissance* **(4)**. Geographically, besides Europe we have included the areas with which medieval Europe came into contact — Iceland, North Africa, the Middle East, Byzantium, and Asia. No particular boundaries have been placed on the subject matter of the individual bibliographies, as long as a meaningful portion of it falls within, or pertains to, the geographic and chronological limits described above. The wide variety of sub-

---

[12] We have included reports of work in progress, the *Bulletin du centre d'information de la recherche d'histoire de France* **(45)** and *Medieval Archaeology* **(132)**; and we have drawn attention to reports of work in progress in the *Répertoire international des médiévistes* **(16)** and the *Bulletin de philosophie médiévale* **(212)**.

ject bibliographies represented indicates the difficulty in delimiting the field.

We have accepted as general principles that, within the boundaries defined above, the guide should be inclusive rather than selective, and that it should describe the bibliographies accurately rather than evaluate them critically. We take it for granted that our readers will recognize that the various bibliographies have set themselves a variety of differing tasks which they perform with widely varying degrees of proficiency. However, since this book is intended not only for professional medievalists but for beginning graduate students as well, we have designated with an asterisk those bibliographies which provide the most thorough and intelligent coverage of their respective fields, from the standpoint of the medievalist. We do not mean to imply that these bibliographies are the only items of value; we merely indicate that they are the obvious ones with which to begin any search of the literature.

The list of serial bibliographies was compiled principally from the major guides to periodicals and bibliographies. Of these, the most useful were Boehm and Adolphus' *Historical Periodicals* [13] and the *Verzeichnis laufend erscheinender Bibliographien*. Also of considerable value were the bibliographic sections of the major serial bibliographies themselves, in particular the *Revue d'histoire ecclésiastique* (141) and the *Jahresberichte für deutsche Geschichte* (62). Father Harold Gardner kindly made available to us the list of bibliographic resources which he compiled for the conference on medieval bibliography held in 1965. Finally, many titles were recommended to us by various colleagues or were discovered by sheer accident. In all, more than 800 titles were examined, and of these, 294 were selected for inclusion.

The serial bibliographies in this guide, numbered consecutively from 1 to 283,[14] are arranged in eleven major divisions and thirty-two subdivisions. Divisions I–III contain the general, regional, and cultural bibliographies; divisions IV–XI contain the subject bibliographies. Within the individual subdivisions the

---

[13] E. H. Boehm and L. Adolphus, eds., *Historical Periodicals* (Santa Barbara, 1961).

[14] Numbers **5, 46, 209, 258,** are duplicates of other items; numbers **32, 88, 146, 202, 223, 245, 276,** each describe two or more bibliographies published in one journal.

bibliographies are listed alphabetically by title. The title of each bibliography is given as it appears on the title page. A bibliography which is a distinct supplement to another publication is entered under its own title. However, if the bibliography is published as an integral part of a journal, it is normally entered under the title of the journal. Following the title we give the publishing institution, place of publication, initial date of publication, and frequency of issue.[15] Where the date of a volume as it appears on the title page differs from the date of publication, both dates are given. Immediately following the heading we note all titles which the bibliography supplements or continues, and significant variations in title. The latter information is not given if it can easily be found in the *Union List of Serials* or *New Serial Titles*.[16]

Each bibliography is accompanied by a descriptive annotation outlining its coverage, organization, and unique features. The annotation first indicates whether articles, books, or both are surveyed in the bibliography, the period and geographic region in which the titles were published, and the subject to which the bibliography is devoted. The annotation next describes the internal organization of the bibliography. In many instances we supplement this description by listing the subject classification of the bibliography itself. Specific features of the bibliography follow, such as the appearance of descriptive and critical annotations, the notation of book reviews, or indexes to the authors, materials and subject matter surveyed in the bibliography. The annotation concludes by indicating when the bibliography began, unless that date is identical with the initial date of publication of the journal itself. Following the annotation, we have noted a recent volume of the bibliography which was examined, and have indicated the approximate lag between the date of coverage and the date of publication, the approximate number of items it contains, and, when ascertainable, the approximate number of journals it attempts to survey. The annotation is an attempt to describe the current appearance of the bibliography. It is, with few exceptions, based on material published between 1964

[15] Editors' names have, as a rule, been omitted except for those bibliographies which are not, strictly speaking, serially published.

[16] *Union List of Serials in Libraries of the United States and Canada,* Edna Brown Titus, ed. (3d ed.; New York, 1965); and *New Serial Titles: A Union List of Serials Commencing Publication after December 31, 1948* (Washington, D.C., 1953–).

and 1967. The annotation's very detail, however, unfortunately insures its obsolescence, because the bibliographies change their organization, periodicity, or coverage with surprising frequency. The subject organization of the guide as a whole is supplemented by cross-references, at the end of each subdivision, to other bibliographies and subdivisions containing relevant material. After careful consideration it was decided that a subject index to the bibliographies included would not significantly increase the accessibility of these items. The work concludes with an index of all titles which appear in the guide, and an index of editors.

We have, from the beginning, benefited from the generous cooperation and support of many individuals and institutions in Europe and North America. We should like in particular to thank J. M. Edelstein, David Farquhar, Andrew Horn, Gerhart Ladner, G. E. von Grunebaum, Lynn White, jr., and Frances Kirschenbaum Zeitlin, of the University of California, Los Angeles; M.-Th. d'Alverny, Centre d'études supérieures de civilisation médiévale, Poitiers; Alex Baer, Universität Konstanz; Giles Barber, Oxford University; Gray C. Boyce, Alameda; H. G. Gardner, C.S.B., University of St. Thomas, Houston; R. W. Hunt, Oxford University; Mary A. Rouse, Los Angeles; André Vernet, École nationale des chartes, Paris; J. F. Zacek, State University of New York at Albany; the Bibliothèque nationale, Paris; the Bodleian Library, Oxford; and the libraries of the following institutions: the Centre d'études supérieures de civilisation médiévale, Poitiers; the Institut de recherche et d'histoire des textes, Paris; Alma College, Los Gatos; the University of California, Berkeley; and, most of all, the University of California, Los Angeles. The completion and publication of this work were made possible by financial assistance from the Grant for International and Comparative Studies of the Ford Foundation, and from the Center for Medieval and Renaissance Studies at the University of California, Los Angeles. We are grateful to S. R. McKernan, A. C. Mooney, and F. H. Sherwood, jr., who helped to prepare the manuscript; and to the University of California Press, which advised us on questions of format and presentation. Especial appreciation is due to Ann Hinckley, of the Research Library of the University of California, Los Angeles, who procured many of these materials for us and graciously shared with us her knowledge of bibliography.

PART ONE

PART ONE

I. General Bibliographies

1. The American Historical Review. (American Historical Association.) New York. 1895–   . Quarterly.

Each number contains an extensive list of articles and of books received, recently published in Europe and North America concerning the general field of history. The publications are classified by geographic area and historical period.

Examined: vol. 71 (1965–66), bibliography for 1964–65, *ca.* 7,000 items.

2. Annual Bulletin of Historical Literature. (Historical Association.) London. 1911–   (publ. 1912–   ). Annual.

Each issue comprises a series of signed bibliographic essays discussing articles and books published during a given year in Europe and North America concerning the history of Europe, North and South America, and the British Empire. The emphasis is on western Europe and Great Britain. Each essay covers a chronological period or general subject. Author index.

Examined: vol. 49 (1963, publ. 1965), bibliography for 1963, *ca.* 750 items.

3. Bibliografia storica nazionale. (Giunta centrale per gli studi storici.) Bari. 1939– (publ. 1942–). Annual.

Each volume comprises an extensive bibliography of articles and books published in Italy during a given year concerning world history, with particular emphasis on Italy, from prehistory to the present. The publications are classified by topic within seven sections: *Scienze ausiliarie e sussidi, Opere di carattere generale, Preistoria, Studia antica, Medioevo, Storia moderna, Storia contemporanea.* Occasional brief descriptive annotations. Reviews are noted (reviews of non-Italian publications are noted only when included in Italian journals). Index of names.

Examined: vol. 25 (1963, publ. 1965), bibliography for 1963, 4,560 items.

*4. Bibliographie internationale de l'humanisme et de la Renaissance. (Fédération internationale des sociétés et instituts pour l'étude de la Renaissance.) Genève. 1965– (publ. 1966–). Annual.

Continues annual "Bibliographie des articles relatifs à l'histoire de l'humanisme et de la Renaissance," published 1948–65 in **Bibliothèque d'humanisme et Renaissance:** Travaux et documents. (Association humanisme et Renaissance.) Genève.

An extensive bibliography of articles and books published during a given year, primarily in Europe and North America, concerning humanism and the Renaissance broadly interpreted to include facets of economics, politics, law, and technology, as well as philosophy, history, religion, and the arts in Europe during the fourteenth, fifteenth, and sixteenth centuries. Books and articles are listed in separate sections, each arranged alphabetically by author. Each volume also will contain a supplement to the previous bibliographies; that in vol. 1 covers 1958–64. Index of authors, places, and subjects.

Examined: vol. 1 (1965, publ. 1966), bibliography for 1965, 3,199 items, *ca.* 750 serials indexed.

5. Bulletin signalétique 19–24: Sciences humaines. (Centre national de la recherche scientifique.) Paris. 1947– . Quarterly.
Entitled **Bulletin analytique: Philosophie,** 1947–55.

The **Bulletin** is an omnicompetent bibliography of periodical publications in the biological and physical sciences and in the humanities. The several bibliographies concerning the social sciences and humanities which comprise sections 19–24 of the **Bulletin** are described herein under their respective individual titles: **19. Philosophie, sciences religieuses (214); 20. Psychologie, pédagogie (205); 21. Sociologie, ethnologie (188); 22. Histoire des sciences et des techniques (274); 23. Littérature et arts du spectacle (230); 24. Sciences du langage (231); Domaines complémentaires (124).**

*6. Cahiers de civilisation médiévale Xᵉ–XIIᵉ siècles. (Centre d'études supérieures de civilisation médiévale, Université de Poitiers.) Poitiers. 1958– . Quarterly.

Each issue contains an extensive bibliography of articles and books recently published, principally in Europe and North America, concerning primarily European history and civilization from the tenth through the twelfth century. To a lesser extent, the bibliography also includes Byzantine, Islamic, and Slavic history and the Middle and Far East. Extensive subject classification in dictionary form with a large number of cross-references. The bibliography is to a degree an index of the major topics discussed in the publications it includes. Reviews are noted. The last issue contains a list of additions to entries in previous volumes, being primarily notices of reviews listed by author being reviewed. Annual author index. Quinquennial indexes of names, places, texts, subjects, and authors reviewed.
Examined: vol. 9 (1966), bibliography for 1963–65, 3,228 items, *ca.* 500 serials indexed.

*7. Deutsches Archiv für Erforschung des Mittelalters. (Monumenta Germaniae Historica.) Köln and Graz. 1937– . Semiannual.
Entitled **Deutsches Archiv für Geschichte des Mittelalters, 1937–44.**

Each issue contains a bibliography of articles and books published recently in Europe and North America concerning medieval studies in general. Classified by topic: *Allgemeines, Hilfswissenschaften und Quellenkunde, Politische und Kirchengeschichte des Mittelalters, Rechts- und Verfassungsgeschichte,*

Sozial- und Wirtschaftsgeschichte, Landeskunde, Kultur- und Geistesgeschichte. Descriptive or critical annotations (up to 200 words). Annual author and subject indexes. Examined: vol. 23 (1967), bibliography for 1965–66, *ca.* 700 items.

8. The English Historical Review. London. 1886– . Quarterly.

The third number of each annual volume contains a select bibliographic survey of "periodical and occasional publications" which appeared during the previous year, principally in Europe and North America, concerning world history from antiquity to the present, with emphasis on western Europe. Brief descriptions of each item are listed chronologically by general topic or major geographic region. The bibliography began in 1924.
Examined: vol. 80 (1965), bibliography for 1964, *ca.* 500 items.

9. Index translationum: Répertoire international des traductions. (UNESCO.) Paris. 1932– . Annual.

Each volume comprises an extensive bibliography of translations published throughout the world during a given year. The publications are classified by country of publication and subdivided according to the Universal Decimal Classification system. Index of authors translated.
Examined: ser. 2, vol. 17 (1964, publ. 1966), bibliography for 1964, 37,167 items.

*10. International Bibliography of Historical Sciences. Internationale Bibliographie der Geschichtswissenschaften. (International Committee of Historical Sciences, Lausanne.) Paris. 1926– (publ. 1930–). Annual.

An extensive bibliography of articles and books published during a given year throughout the world concerning history and the historical sciences. Classified by historical period, geographic area, and topic. Major sections are devoted to auxiliary sciences (including paleography, diplomatics, history of the book, chronology, genealogy, sigillography and heraldry, numismatics, linguistics, historical geography, and iconography), the patristic period, Byzantine history, and the Middle Ages (including sources, general studies, political history, the Jews, Islam, the Vikings, law and institutions, economics and society, intellectual history, art, music, philosophy, ecclesiastical history, and population). Reviews are noted. Name and geographic indexes. Bibliography for 1940–46 has not been published.

Examined: vol. 32 (1963, publ. 1966), bibliography for 1963, 7,874 items, *ca.* 2,900 serials indexed.

*11. International Guide to Medieval Studies: A Quarterly Index to Periodical Literature. (American Bibliographic Service.) Darien, Connecticut. 1961– . Quarterly.

Each issue comprises a list of articles recently published, principally in Europe and North America, concerning all aspects of the Middle Ages, with emphasis on western Europe from the sixth to the fourteenth century. The publications are listed alphabetically by author. Frequent brief descriptive annotations. Extensive subject index, cumulated annually. Annual author index.

Examined: vol. 5 (1965–66), bibliography for 1964–65, 802 items.

*12. International Medieval Bibliography. (Department of History, University of Minnesota.) Minneapolis. 1967– . Five issues of cards yearly.

An extensive bibliography of articles and books recently published throughout the world concerning "the history and civilization of Europe from the accession of Diocletian to the end of the fifteenth century," including art, numismatics, theology, literature, and Byzantine studies. The bibliography is issued on index cards to permit interfiling. The cards are arranged alphabetically by author, with subject headings to allow refiling by country or geographic region, subdivided by general topic. Four issues are devoted to articles appearing in a select list of journals, the fifth to books reviewed in these journals. Reviews are noted. Quarterly subject index, the fourth being an annual cumulation. Beginning with 1968–69, a considerably enlarged **I.M.B.** will be compiled in cooperation with the **MLA International Bibliography (232);** and the **I.M.B.** will be published in book form.

Examined: 1967 (publ. 1967–68), bibliography for 1967, *ca.* 1,500 items, 148 serials indexed.

*13. Quarterly Check-List of Medievalia: An International Index of Current Books, Monographs, Brochures & Separates. (American Bibliographic Service.) Darien, Connecticut. 1958– . Quarterly.

Each issue comprises a list of books recently published in Europe and North America concerning all aspects of Europe and Byzantium from the fourth through the fifteenth century. Publications are listed alphabetically by author. Directory of publishers. Annual author index.

Examined: vol. 9 (1966), bibliography for 1964–65, 806 items.

14. Quarterly Check-List of Renaissance Studies: An International Index of Current Books, Monographs, Brochures & Separates. (American Bibliographic Service.) Darien, Connecticut. 1959– . Quarterly.

Each issue comprises a list of books recently published in Europe and North America concerning European history from the fifteenth to the seventeenth century. Publications are listed alphabetically by author. Annual directory of publishers and author index.

Examined: vol. 7 (1965), bibliography for 1964–65, 381 items.

15. Renaissance Quarterly. (Renaissance Society of America.) New York. 1948– . Quarterly.
Entitled **Renaissance News,** 1948–66.

Each issue contains a bibliography of books recently published, principally in Europe and North America, concerning various facets of the Renaissance. Publications are classified by topic. Occasional brief descriptive annotations. In addition, this journal occasionally contains signed bibliographic essays discussing recent publication on a given topic in Renaissance studies, e.g. *History, Art, English Literature.* The bibliography began in 1952.

Examined: vol. 20 (1967), bibliography for 1965–66, *ca.* 1,000 items.

*16. Répertoire international des médiévistes. (Centre d'études supérieures de civilisation médiévale, Université de Poitiers.) Poitiers. 1965– . Quinquennial.

Supplement to **Cahiers de civilisation médiévale.** (Centre d'études supérieures de civilisation médiévale, Université de Poitiers.) Poitiers. Continues **Répertoire des médiévistes européens,** supplement to **Cahiers de civilisation médiévale.** Poitiers. 1960. And **Répertoire des médiévistes d'Europe,** supplement to **Mélanges de science religieuse.** Paris and Tournai. 1954.

An alphabetical register of scholars throughout the world who work in the numerous disciplines of medieval studies. The following information is provided for each individual: name, position, address, fields of interest or specialization, publications during the previous five years (excluding book reviews), and works currently in preparation. The **Répertoire** is largely dependent for its information upon the response of the individual medievalists included. It provides a broad and detailed picture of current publication and research by the international community of medievalists. Indexes of places of residence and of fields of interest or specialization. This information was formerly provided for American and Canadian medievalists by **Progress of Medieval and Renaissance Studies in the United States and Canada.** S. H. Thomson, ed. Boulder, Colorado. 1923–60. Examined: vol. 1 (1965), publications for 1959–64, 3,530 medievalists.

17. Revue historique. Paris. 1876– . Quarterly.

Each issue contains several bibliographic sections which togather report recent periodical and monographic publication in Europe and North America concerning ancient, medieval, and modern history. The two principal ones are "Bulletin historique," an extensive signed critical review of research and publication in a significant historical endeavor during a given period; and "Recueils périodiques et sociétés savantes," a list of select articles from major Western historical journals classified by historical period and topic, with occasional brief descriptive annotations. These two sections are complemented by critical reviews and short notices of recent monographic publication. Semiannual index of authors of books.

Examined: vols. 231–232 (1964), bibliography for 1963–64, *ca.* 1,000 items ("Recueils" only).

18. Speculum: A Journal of Mediaeval Studies. (Mediaeval Academy of America.) Cambridge, Massachusetts. 1926– . Quarterly.

Each issue contains a brief bibliography of articles published recently in North America concerning medieval culture and society in Europe and the Middle East. Publications are classified by topic. The bibliography began in 1934.
Examined: vol. 41 (1966), bibliography for 1965–66, *ca.* 225 items.

19. Tijdschrift voor Geschiedenis. Groningen. 1886– . Quarterly.

Each issue normally contains two bibliographies of articles and books recently published in Europe and North America concerning history in general from antiquity to the present. The first bibliography is devoted to articles; the second to monographic publications. Each is classified by historical period, subdivided by country or geographic area. The bibliography of monographic publications began in 1920; the bibliography of articles began in 1964.
Examined: vol. 79 (1966), bibliography for 1965–66, *ca.* 1,750 items.

20. Zeitschrift für Geschichtswissenschaft. Berlin. 1953– . Eight issues yearly.

Four of the eight numbers in each annual volume normally contain a bibliography of articles recently published in Europe and North America concerning German and world history, from antiquity to the present. The publications are classified by historical period. This bibliography complements a large section devoted to reviews and short notices of current books.
Examined: vol. 13 (1965), bibliography for 1964–65, *ca.* 1,250 items.

See also:

II. National and Regional Bibliographies

A. Asia

21. Annual Bibliography of Oriental Studies. Tōyōgaku bunken ruimoku. (Research Institute for Humanistic Studies, Kyoto University.) Kyoto. 1934– (publ. 1935–). Annual.

An extensive bibliography of articles and books published during a given year in Europe, North America, the Soviet Union, and the Far East concerning the social and cultural history of the Orient, Central Asia, and the Middle East. The bibliography is divided into two major parts: publications in Japanese and Chinese, and publications in the roman and cyrillic alphabets (subdivided into articles and books). Each part is classified into the following subjects: *History, Geography, Social Studies, Economics, Politics, Law and Institutions, Religion, Philosophy* . . . , *Science, Literature, Art, Archaeology, Inscriptions and Palaeography, Ethnography, Philology, Bibliography, Series* . . . , *Chronicle (Obituary).* Material is included on economic, cultural, religious, and technological interaction between the Orient and the West and the Moslem world. Book reviews are noted. Indexes of authors in Japanese and Chinese and the roman alphabet and the cyrillic alphabet. Non-Oriental publication has been included beginning with the volume for 1946–50. One special number has been published, **Mōko kenkyū bunken ruimoku. Bibliography of Mongolia for 1900–1950,** I. Shinobu and F. Akīra, eds., 1953.

Examined: 1964 (publ. 1967), bibliography for 1964, 5,950 Eastern items, *ca.* 375 Eastern serials indexed; 6,296 Western items, *ca.* 103 Western serials indexed.

22. **The Journal of Asian Studies.** (Association for Asian Studies.) Ann Arbor, Michigan. 1941–   . Five issues yearly.

Entitled **The Far Eastern Quarterly,** 1941–55.

Continues **Bulletin of Far Eastern Bibliography.** (Committee on Far Eastern Bibliography, American Council of Learned Societies.) Washington, D.C. 1936–40.

The last issue of each annual volume comprises the "Bibliography of Asian Studies," an extensive bibliography of articles and books published throughout the world during the previous year concerning the broad area of Asian studies. The bibliography is classified by country or geographic region. Each section is subdivided into the following topics: *Periodicals, General and Miscellaneous, Philosophy and Religion, History, Geography, Economics, Science, Politics, Government, Education, Music, Arts, Language and Literature.* While the emphasis of the bibliography is on the contemporary period, material relevant to medieval Europe is included in the historical sections. Occasional brief descriptive annotations. Titles in non-roman alphabets are transliterated. Author index.

Examined: vol. 24 (1965), bibliography for 1964, *ca.* 10,000 items.

23. **Orientalistische Literaturzeitung:** Monatsschrift für die Wissenschaft vom ganzen Orient und seinen Beziehungen zu den angrenzenden Kulturkreisen. (Deutsche Akademie der Wissenschaften zu Berlin.) Berlin and Leipzig. 1898–   . Six issues yearly.

Each issue contains a survey of recent periodical and monographic publications, primarily from Europe, the Middle East and North America, in the field of oriental studies including the ancient Middle East, Jewish, Islamic, and Asian history. The survey is divided into three parts: a critical review article, reviews of recent books arranged by subject, and a collection of tables of contents of recent issues of major journals in the field. The articles listed in the latter are frequently supplied with brief descriptive annotations.

Examined: vol. 61 (1966), bibliography for 1965, 184 reviews, 47 periodical titles surveyed.

24. Revue bibliographique de sinologie. (École pratique des hautes études, VIᵉ section.) Paris and 's-Gravenhage. 1955– (publ. 1957–). Annual.

Each annual volume comprises a bibliography of articles and books recently published, primarily in China and Japan, but also in Europe and North America, concerning all aspects of the history of China, from antiquity through the present. Publications are classified by general subject, subdivided by historical period. There are sections on bibliography, history and the social sciences, archaeology and art, language, literature, music, philosophy and religion, and the history of science. Material is included on contacts with the Western world. Signed descriptive or critical annotations (up to 500 words) in French or English. Author and subject indexes.

Examined: vol. 5 (1959, publ. 1965), bibliography for 1959, 862 items, *ca.* 75 serials indexed.

25. Ural-altaische Jahrbücher: Internationale Zeitschrift für uralische und altaische Forschung. (Societas Uralo-Altaica.) Wiesbaden. 1921– . Semiannual.
   Entitled **Ungarische Jahrbücher,** 1921–43.

Each issue normally contains a bibliography of articles and books recently published, primarily in Germany, Hungary, and Finland, concerning Uralic and Altaic philology. The bibliography normally is divided into two parts. One part is devoted to Uralic philology, including Magyar, Ob-Ugrian, Baltic Sea Finnish, Lapp, Volga Finnish, Permian, and Samoyed. The other is devoted to Altaic philology, including Turkic, Mongolic, and Tungusic. Initialed descriptive or critical annotations (up to 500 words). Index of names. Bibliography began in 1952 (for 1945–51).

Examined: vol. 36 (1965), bibliography for 1962–63, 54 items (Uralic bibliography only).

B. Belgium, the Netherlands, and Luxembourg

26. **Bibliographie luxembourgeoise.** (Bibliothèque nationale, Luxembourg.) Luxembourg. 1944– (publ. 1945–). Annual.

A bibliography of articles, maps, books, and records acquired during a given year by the national library which were either published in Luxembourg, written by Luxembourgers, or devoted to the grand duchy of Luxembourg. The bibliography is thus largely devoted to historical and contemporary aspects of the grand duchy. The publications are classified by subject. Occasional brief descriptive annotations. Indexes of authors, general subjects, and of subjects concerning Luxembourg.
Examined: vol. 20 (1964, publ. 1965), bibliography for 1964, 755 items.

27. **Bijdragen voor de Geschiedenis der Nederlanden.** 's-Gravenhage and Antwerpen. 1946– . Quarterly.
Continues the bibliography published 1901–44 in **Bijdragen voor Vaderlandsche Geschiedenis en Oudheidkunde.** Arnhem and 's-Gravenhage.

One number of each annual volume contains a "kroniek" or bibliographic essay discussing articles and books recently published, principally in the Netherlands, concerning the general history of the Netherlands up to the present. The descriptions or annotations (up to 500 words) are grouped by major chronological period.
Examined: vol. 21 (1966–67), bibliography for 1965–66, *ca.* 350 items.

28. **Bulletin bibliographique d'histoire liégeoise.** (Commission belge de bibliographie.) Bruxelles. 1944– (publ. 1948–). Irregular.
Reprinted from **Annuaire d'histoire liégeoise.** (Commission communale de l'histoire de l'ancien pays de Liège.) Liège.

Each volume comprises a bibliography of articles and books published during a given period, principally in the Low Countries, concerning the history of Liège and its environs from antiquity to the present. The publications are listed alphabetically by author. Occasional descriptive annotations (up to 75 words). Reviews are noted. Subject index.
Examined: vol. 6 (1963–65, publ. 1966), bibliography for 1963–65, 2,786 items.

29. Handelingen van het Genootschap voor Geschiedenis Gesticht onder de Benaming Société d'émulation te Brugge. Annales de la Société d'émulation de Bruges. (Société d'émulation de Bruges.) Bruges. 1839– . Annual.

Each volume contains a bibliography of articles recently published, primarily in Belgium, concerning the history of the county of Flanders and the province of West Flanders. The publications are classified by topic under three major headings: *Hulpwetenschappen, Algemene Geschiedenis,* and *Bizjondere Geschiedenis.* Occasional descriptive annotations (up to 50 words). Author index. The bibliography began in 1951.
Examined: vol. 102 (1965, publ. 1966), bibliography for 1965, 313 items.

*30. Repertorium van Boeken en Tijdschriftartikelen betreffende de Geschiedenis van Nederland. (Nederlands Comité voor geschiedkundige Wetenschappen.) Leiden. 1940– (publ. 1943–). Triennial.
Continues **Repertorium der Verhandelingen en Bijdragen betreffende de Geschiedenis des Vaderlands.** Leiden. 1863–1939 (publ. 1907–53).

Each volume comprises an extensive bibliography of articles and books published during a given period, principally in Europe and North America, concerning the history of the Netherlands from antiquity to the present. Publications are classified by topic, historical period, and geographic area under eleven major headings: *Algemeen, Depôts, Organisatie; Hulpwetenschappen; Geschiedenis van Nederland naar Tijdvakken; Gewestelijke en plaatselijke Geschiedenis; Waterstaatsgeschiedenis; Koloniale Geschiedenis van Nederland; Maritieme en militaire Geschiedenis;*

Economische en sociale Geschiedenis; Rechtsgeschiedenis van Nederland; Kerkgeschiedenis van Nederland; Cultuurgeschiedenis van Nederland. Occasional brief descriptive annotations. Reviews are noted. Indexes of authors, persons, and places. Examined: 1954–56 (publ. 1963), bibliography for 1954–56, 4,392 items.

*31. Revue belge de philologie et d'histoire. Belgisch Tijdschrift voor Filologie en Geschiedenis. (Société pour le progrès des études philologiques et historiques.) Bruxelles. 1922– . Quarterly.

The fourth number of each annual volume contains the "Bibliographie de l'histoire de Belgique," which includes articles and books published during the previous year in Europe and North America concerning the history of Belgium from antiquity to the present. The publications are classified by topic under three major headings: *Bibliographies et sciences auxiliaires, Travaux généraux,* and *Histoire par époques.* The last is subdivided by chronological period and also contains sections devoted to individual geographic areas. Occasional brief descriptive annotations. The bibliography first appeared in this journal in 1953. Bibliographies for 1944–51 were published in **Revue du Nord (32),** 1947–52.
Examined: vol. 42 (1964), bibliography for 1963, 1,283 items.

32. Revue du Nord: Revue historique trimestrielle, Nord de la France — Belgique — Pays-Bas (Faculté des lettres et sciences humaines, Université de Lille.) Lille. 1910– . Quarterly.

Each annual volume normally contains two bibliographies, "Bulletin d'histoire de Belgique" and "Bulletin critique de l'historiographie néerlandaise." Each comprises a series of bibliographic essays surveying articles and books published during a given period, principally in Europe, concerning the history of its respective country from antiquity to the present. Each individual essay treats a given historical period and is subdivided by topic. The bibliography for Belgium began in 1953; that for the Netherlands began in 1954. Between 1947 and 1952 this journal con-

tained the "Bibliographie de l'histoire de Belgique" now published in **Revue belge de philologie et d'histoire (31)**.
Examined: vol. 46 (1964), bibliographies for 1962–63, 221 items.

See also:
   120. **Artes textiles**
   129. **Helinium**
   156. **Archief voor de Geschiedenis van de Katholieke Kerk in Nederland**
   163. **Hansische Geschichtsblätter**
   183. **Répertoire bibliographique du droit belge**
   245. **Handelingen van de Koninklijke Commissie voor Toponymie & Dialectologie**
   282. **Scientiarum historia**

C. British Isles

33. **Bibliotheca Celtica:** A Register of Publications Relating to Wales and the Celtic Peoples & Languages. (National Library of Wales.) Aberystwyth. 1909–   (publ. 1910–   ). Annual.

A bibliography of articles and books published during a given year in Europe and North America concerning the Celtic languages, literature, religion, and history. The publications are arranged according to the Library of Congress subject classification. Index of names.
Examined: 1963 (publ. 1965), bibliography for 1963, *ca.* 1,250 items.

34. **Irish Historical Studies.** (Irish Historical Society. Ulster Society for Irish Historical Studies.) Dublin. 1938–   . Semiannual.

The second and fourth numbers of each biennial volume contain "Writings on Irish History," a bibliography of articles and books published during the previous year in Europe and North America concerning Irish history from antiquity to the present. The publications are arranged in three sections: *Sources and Guides, Secondary Works*, and *Addenda* to previous years. Oc-

18   SERIAL BIBLIOGRAPHIES

casional brief descriptive annotations. The bibliography began in 1942.

Examined: vol. 14 (1964–65), bibliographies for 1963 and 1964, *ca.* 600 items.

35. The Scottish Historical Review. Edinburgh. 1903– . Semi-annual.

The second number of each annual volume contains a bibliography of articles published during the previous year in Scotland, Europe, and North America concerning Scottish history from antiquity to the present. Classified by historical period, e.g. *Dark Ages to 1100; Middle Ages: 1100 to 1560.* Occasional brief descriptive annotations. The bibliography began in 1960.

Examined: vol. 43 (1964), bibliography for 1963, *ca.* 150 items.

*36. Writings on British History. A. T. Milne, ed. (Institute of Historical Research, University of London.) London. 1934– (publ. 1937–). Irregular.

Each volume comprises an extensive bibliography of articles and books published during a given period, throughout the world, concerning the history of Great Britain from *ca.* 400 to 1914. Publications on the local history of the English fiefs in France and the domestic history of the Commonwealth countries are omitted except when they directly concern English history. The bibliography is in two sections: *General Works,* classified by topic, and *Period Histories,* classified by chronological period and subdivided by topic. Occasional brief descriptive annotations. Reviews are noted. Author and subject index. **Writings on British History** is complemented by the Institute's **Bibliography of Historical Works Issued in the United Kingdom: 1946–56,** J. C. Lancaster, ed., 1957; **1957–60,** W. Kellaway, ed., 1962; **1961–65,** W. Kellaway, ed., 1967.

Examined: 1940–45 (publ. 1960), bibliography for 1940–45, 2 vols., 12,380 items.

See also:
2. Annual Bulletin of Historical Literature
    117. Archaeological Bibliography for Great Britain & Ireland

132. **Medieval Archaelogy**
160. **The Agricultural History Review**
162. **The Economic History Review**
238. **Abstracts of English Studies**
240. **American Speech**
241. **Annual Bibliography of English Language and Literature**
250. **The Year's Work in English Studies**
280. **The Journal of Transport History**

D. France

37. **Annales de Normandie.** (Société d'enquêtes ethnographiques.) Caen. 1951– . Quarterly.

Continues "Bulletin bibliographique et critique d'histoire de Normandie" published 1928–39 in **Normannia:** Revue bibliographique et critique d'histoire de Normandie. (Société des antiquaires de Normandie.) Caen.

And **Bulletin bibliographique et critique d'histoire de Normandie.** (Société bibliographique d'histoire de Normandie.) Caen. 1925–27.

One number of each annual volume comprises the "Bibliographie normande," which contains articles and books published during the previous year in Europe and North America concerning the history of the Normans and Normandy from antiquity to the present. Publications dealing with northern Gaul, the Viking movements, and Norman Sicily and southern Italy are included. Classified by general topic; subdivided by subject or chronological period. Occasional brief descriptive annotations. Reviews are noted. Author index. This bibliography is also published in **Cahiers Léopold Delisle (46).**

Examined: vol. 15 (1965), bibliography for 1964, 622 items.

38. **Annales du Midi:** Revue archéologique, historique et philologique de la France méridionale. Toulouse. 1889– . Quarterly.

The last number of each annual volume normally contains the "Bibliographie de la France méridionale," which includes articles and books published during the previous year in Europe

and North America concerning the history and civilization of southern France from antiquity to the present. Classified in two sections: *Les civilisations de la France méridionale* (subdivided by subject) and *L'évolution de la France méridionale* (subdivided by historical period). The bibliography began in 1949.
Examined: vol. 77 (1965), bibliography for 1964, 1,585 items.

*39. Bibliographie annuelle de l'histoire de France du cinquième siècle à 1945. (Comité français des sciences historiques.) Paris. 1955– (publ. 1956–). Annual.
Continues **Répertoire bibliographique de l'histoire de France.** (Société française de bibliographie.) Paris. 1920–31 (publ. 1923–38).

An extensive bibliography of articles and books published during a given year in Europe and North America concerning French history and civilization from the fifth century to 1945. The publications are classified by topic and historical period within eight major sections: *Manuels généraux et sciences auxiliaires de l'histoire, Histoire politique de la France, Histoire des institutions, Histoire économique et sociale, Histoire religieuse, La France outre-mer, Histoire de la civilisation, Histoire locale.* Brief descriptive annotations. Extensive subject and author indexes. It is the intention of the Comité to complete the bibliography for the years 1932–54; the first volume covering the years 1953–54 appeared in 1964.
Examined: 1964 (publ. 1965), bibliography for 1964, 9,414 items, *ca.* 1,250 serials indexed.

40. Bibliographie bourguignonne: Bulletin des publications historiques récentes. (Centre d'études bourguignonnes.) Dijon. 1952– . Annual.
Published as a separately paginated supplement in **Annales de Bourgogne:** Revue historique trimestrielle. (Centre d'études bourguignonnes.) Dijon.
Continues "Bibliographie bourguignonne" in **Annales de Bourgogne,** 1939–51.

Each issue normally comprises half of a biennial bibliography of articles and books published during a given two-year period in Europe and North America concerning the duchy and county of Burgundy from antiquity to the present. Classified by topic and historical period. Occasional brief descriptive annotations. Reviews are noted.

Examined: ser. 11 (1962–63, publ. 1963–64), bibliography for 1962–63, 624 items; in **Annales de Bourgogne,** vols. 35–36 (1963–64).

41. Bibliographie lorraine. (Faculté des lettres, Université de Nancy. Fédération historique lorraine.) Nancy. 1909– (publ. 1910–   ). Annual.

Published in **Annales de l'Est.** (Faculté des lettres, Université de Nancy. Fédération historique lorraine.) Nancy.

A bibliography of articles and books published during the previous year in Europe and North America concerning the history of Lorraine. Classified according to general topic and chronological period. Frequent brief descriptive annotations. Reviews are noted. Author and subject index. Bibliography was not published during the years 1940–51 (for 1938–50).

Examined: vol. 31 (1964, publ. 1965), bibliography for 1964, 666 items.

42. Bulletin. (Fédération des sociétés historiques et archéologiques de Paris et de l'Île-de-France.) 1960–   . Biennial.

Each issue comprises the "Bibliographie analytique des publications d'histoire et d'archéologie concernant Paris et la région parisienne," which contains articles and books published during a given year, primarily in France, concerning all aspects of the history and archaeology of Paris and the Île-de-France from prehistory through the present. Publications are classified by general subject: *Instruments de travail et sciences auxiliaires d'histoire, Histoire et archéologie par époques et par lieux, Histoire par spécialités.* Each of these is extensively subdivided by topic or historical period. Descriptive annotations (up to 50 words). Subject and author indexes. Vol. 1 of the **Bulletin** was a guide to local scholarly societies, "Les sociétés savantes de la région parisienne." The bibliography began with vol. 2 (1961–62, publ. 1963).

Examined: vol. 3 (1963–64, publ. 1966), bibliography for 1962, 1,033 items.

43. Bulletin de la Société archéologique et historique du Limousin. (Société archéologique et historique du Limousin.) Limoges. 1846– . Annual.

Each volume contains the "Notes bibliographiques relatives au Limousin (Corrèze, Creuse, Haute-Vienne)," which includes articles, books, and catalogs of sales and expositions published during a given period, primarily in Europe, concerning the culture, history, and geography of the Limousin. Publications are classified under five major headings: *Généralités* (including museums, exhibits, and auctions), *Archéologie et histoire de l'art* (subdivided by historical period with sections devoted to enamel and gold, tapestries, and ceramics), *Histoire* (subdivided by historical period), *Disciplines spéciales* (including biography, literature, linguistics, music, folklore), *Géographie-Civilisation* (including cartography and physical, human, and economic geography). Frequent brief descriptive annotations. Bibliography began in 1954.

Examined: vol. 93 (1966), bibliography for 1964–65, 336 items.

44. Bulletin de la Société des antiquaires de Normandie. (Société des antiquaires de Normandie.) Caen. 1860– . Annual.

Each annual volume contains the "Chronique d'archéologie normande," which comprises a bibliography of articles and books published in western Europe during the previous year concerning the archaeology and history of Normandy from antiquity to 1789. Following a section devoted to general studies, the publications are classified by chronological period according to the major *départements* of Normandy: Manche, Orne, Calvados, Eure, and Seine-Maritime. Brief descriptive annotations. Bibliography began in vol. 53 (1955–56, publ. 1957).

Examined: vol. 57 (1963–64, publ. 1965), bibliography for 1963–64, 387 items.

45. Bulletin du Centre d'information de la recherche d'histoire de France. (Centre d'information de la recherche d'histoire de France, Archives nationales.) Paris. 1953– . Semiannual.

Each issue comprises an extensive list of research in progress, including doctoral dissertations, by Frenchmen and others concerning the history of France. The list is classified according to ten major topics: *Sciences auxiliaires de l'histoire; Histoire diplomatique, étrangère et coloniale; Histoire générale de la France; Histoire de Paris; Histoire provinciale; Histoire économique et sociale; Histoire du droit et des institutions; Histoire religieuse; Histoire de la civilisation; Biographies.* Indexes of authors (including mailing addresses) and subjects.
    Examined: vol. 11 (1963, publ. 1965), research in progress for 1962–63, 1,551 items.

46. Cahiers Léopold Delisle. (Société parisienne d'histoire et d'archéologic normandes.) Paris. 1947– . Quarterly.

Beginning in 1958, the first number of each annual volume has contained the "Bibliographie normande," which is also published in **Annales de Normandie (37).**

47. French Historical Studies. (Society for French Historical Studies, North Carolina State College.) Raleigh, North Carolina. 1958– . Semiannual.

Each issue contains a bibliography of books recently published, principally in France, concerning French history from antiquity to the present. Publications are classified by historical period.
    Examined: vol. 4 (1965–66), bibliography for 1963–66, *ca.* 1,000 items.

48. Revue d'Alsace. (Institut des hautes études alsaciennes. Fédération des sociétés d'histoire et d'archéologie d'Alsace.) Strasbourg and Colmar. 1850– . Annual.
    Bibliography is continued from **Bibliographie alsacienne:** Revue critique des publications concernant l'Alsace. (Faculté des Lettres de l'Université de Strasbourg.) Strasbourg. 1918–36 (publ. 1922–38).

Each annual volume contains the "Bibliographie alsacienne," which includes articles and books published during the preceding year, principally in France, concerning primarily the history of Alsatian culture, economy, society, and art. Classified by

topic within broad chronological sections. Occasional brief descriptive annotations. Author index. Bibliography began in 1947 (for 1940).
Examined: vol. 103 (1965), bibliography for 1962–64, 1,138 items.

See also:
158. **Revue d'histoire de l'église de France**
177. **Bibliographie en langue française d'histoire du droit**
187. **Arts et traditions populaires**
255. **Bibliographie der französischen Literaturwissenschaft**
256. **Bulletin bibliographique de la Société Rencesvals**
266. **Studi francesi**

E. Germany, Austria, and Switzerland

49. **Bayerische Bibliographie.** (Kommission für bayerische Landesgeschichte. Generaldirektion der bayerischen staatlichen Bibliotheken.) München. 1966– . Irregular.
Supplement to **Zeitschrift für bayerische Landesgeschichte.** (Kommission für bayerische Landesgeschichte, Bayerische Akademie der Wissenschaften. Gesellschaft für fränkische Geschichte.)
Continues annual bibliography published 1928–61 in **Zeitschrift für bayerische Landesgeschichte.**

An extensive bibliography of articles and books published during a given period, primarily in Germany, concerning all aspects, historical and contemporary, of Bavaria. The publications are classified within four major sections: I. *Gesamt-Bayern (Landes- und Volkskunde, Geschichte, Kriegs- und Heerwesen, Genealogie und Heraldik, Münzenwesen, Recht, Wirtschaft und Wirtschaftsgeschichte, Verkehr, Medizin, Kirche, Schule, Kunst, Buchkunst und Bibliotheken, Geistigesleben)*; II. *Einzelne Landesteile* (subdivided by geographic region); III. *Orte und Landkreise*; IV. *Personen und Familien.* The bibliography was formerly devoted primarily to history and included Franconia, Swabia, and the Palatinate. Author index.
Examined: vol. 1 (1959–63, publ. 1966), bibliography for 1959–63, 7,248 items.

50. Bibliographie der Schweizergeschichte. Bibliographie de l'histoire suisse. (Schweizerische Landesbibliothek.) Bern. 1913– (publ. 1914–). Annual.
   Supplement 1921–39 to **Zeitschrift für schweizerische Geschichte.** (Allgemeine geschichtforschende Gesellschaft der Schweiz.) Zürich. And 1914–20 to **Anzeiger für schweizerische Geschichte.** (A.G.G.S.) Bern.
   Continues **Bibliographie der schweizer Geschichte.** Hans Barth, ed. 3 vols. Basel. 1914–15. Supplement **(Handbuch)** to **Quellen zur schweizer Geschichte.** (A.G.G.S.) Basel.

An extensive bibliography of articles and books published during a given year in Europe and North America concerning the history of Switzerland and the Swiss people from antiquity to the present. Publications are classified in two sections, by historical period and by topic. Brief descriptive annotations. Author and subject index.
   Examined: 1964 (publ. 1965), bibliography for 1964, 2,347 items.

51. Bibliographie zur schleswig-holsteinischen Geschichte und Landeskunde. Neumünster. 1928– (publ. 1936–). Annual.
   Supplement to **Zeitschrift der Gesellschaft für schleswig-holsteinische Geschichte.** (Gesellschaft für schleswig-holsteinische Geschichte.) Neumünster.

Each volume comprises an extensive bibliography of articles and books published during a given period, principally in Denmark and Germany, concerning the natural and social history of Schleswig-Holstein. The publications are classified by general topic, subdivided by subject, historical period, and geographic area. Reviews are noted. Author and subject indexes.
   Examined: vol. 6 (1955–60, publ. 1964–65), bibliography for 1955–60, 6,635 items.

52. Blätter für deutsche Landesgeschichte. (Gesamtverein der deutschen Geschichts- und Altertumsvereine.) Wiesbaden. 1852– . Annual.

Each volume contains an extensive bibliographic survey in two parts for recent German, Austrian, and Swiss publications concerning state and local history in those countries. The first part contains tables of contents of state and local historical journals arranged by geographic region. The second contains signed critical reviews of up to 2,500 words for significant books and signed bibliographic essays discussing both articles and books concerning a given topic in German history. The reviews and essays are arranged in two sections: general history, subdivided by topic, and local history, subdivided by geographic and political region. The survey concludes with a list of current publications which will be reviewed in the coming volume. Author and subject indexes for part two. The survey began in 1936 and assumed its present form in 1951.

Examined: vol. 100 (1964), bibliography for 1963–64; part 1, *ca.* 250 journals; part 2, 809 items.

53. Braunschweigisches Jahrbuch. (Braunschweigischer Geschichtsverein.) Braunschweig and Wolfenbüttel. 1902– . Annual.

Each issue contains the "Bibliographie zur braunschweigischen Landesgeschichte," which includes articles and books published during a given year, primarily in Germany, concerning all aspects of the history and culture of Braunschweig, from prehistory to the present. The publications are classified by general subject, e.g. *Kirchengeschichte, Wirtschafts- und Verkehrsgeschichte, Bevölkerungs- und Personengeschichte.* Occasional brief descriptive annotations. Bibliography began in 1955.

Examined: vol. 46 (1965), bibliography for 1964, 334 items.

54. Bremisches Jahrbuch. (Historische Gesellschaft zu Bremen.) Bremen. 1864– . Annual.

Each annual volume contains a critical bibliographic essay surveying articles and books recently published, primarily in Germany, concerning the history of Bremen and its hinterland. The publications are discussed under the following headings: *Allgemeines — Bibliographisches und Hilfswissenschaftliches, Vor- und Frühgeschichte, Mittel- und Nachmittelalter, Hansisches und Hanseatisches, Rechtsgeschichtliches, Geistesgeschichte . . . , Wirtschaftsgeschichte . . . , Sozialgeschichte, Ortsgeschichtliches, Sprache und Volkskunde, Familien- und Personengeschichte.* Bibliography began in 1939.

Examined: vol. 49 (1964), bibliography for 1963, *ca.* 150 items.

55. Bulletin bibliographique de l'Institut historique allemand à Paris. (Institut historique allemand à Paris). Paris. 1962– . Three issues yearly.

Each issue comprises a list of current monographic acquisitions of the Institut, namely books recently published in Germany concerning all aspects of German history. The publications are classified within several sections, including one devoted to local history which is subdivided by region and another devoted to German history which is subdivided by chronological period. In addition, there are extensive sections containing tables of contents of festschriften, certain monographic series, and periodicals. Occasional descriptive annotations (up to 150 words) for periodical articles only. Annual author index.
Examined: nos. 16–18 (1967), bibliography for 1966, 335 items, 74 festschriften and periodicals.

56. Geschichte in Wissenschaft und Unterricht. (Verband der Geschichtslehrer Deutschlands.) Stuttgart. 1950– . Monthly.

Each issue contains a bibliographic survey of articles and books recently published in Germany concerning a broad period or aspect of German history, e.g. ancient, medieval, and reformation history, ecclesiastical, economic, and art history. Each topic normally appears biennially. The survey for the Middle Ages contains several sections on German history, also English history, constitutional history, and art history.
Examined: vol. 15 (1964), bibliography for 1962–63, 667 items.

57. Jahrbuch der Albertus-Universität zu Königsberg, Preussen. (Albertus-Universität zu Königsberg, Preussen.) Würzburg. 1951– . Annual.

Each volume contains the annual "Ostdeutsche Bibliographie," an extensive bibliography of articles and books published during a given year, primarily in West Germany, concerning the German East-Elbian territories. Emphasis is placed on the

"Central-European Problem," especially since World War II. The publications are classified by general subject, often subdivided by geographic region. The medieval portion of the historical section is subdivided into general studies, Baltic area, Prussia, Pomerania, Brandenburg, Silesia, Bohemia and Moravia, Poland and Russia, and southeastern Europe. Triennial author and subject index. The bibliography began in 1952 (for 1945–48).
  Examined: vol. 16 (1966), bibliography for 1964, *ca.* 2,500 items.

58. Jahrbuch der Wittheit zu Bremen. Bremen. 1957– . Annual.

Each volume contains a bibliography of articles and books published in Germany during a given two-year period concerning all aspects of the history of Bremen, with emphasis on the present. Publications are classified by general subject. Occasional brief descriptive annotations.
  Examined: vol. 7 (1963), bibliography for 1961–62, *ca.* 350 items.

59. Jahrbuch des Historischen Vereins für Mittelfranken. (Historischer Verein für Mittelfranken.) Ansbach. 1830– . Biennial.

Each annual volume contains the "Literaturschau für Mittelfranken," which surveys articles and books recently published, primarily in Germany, concerning the history and culture of middle Franconia from antiquity to the present. The bibliography is divided into three parts: initialed critical reviews; contents of periodicals pertaining to middle Franconia, alphabetically arranged by periodical title; and articles in journals devoted to local history, alphabetically arranged by town and region. The bibliography began in 1959.
  Examined: vol. 82 (1964–65), bibliography for 1963–64, 32 reviews, 77 journals.

60. Jahrbuch für die Geschichte Mittel- und Ostdeutschlands. (Historische Kommission zu Berlin. Friedrich-Meinecke-Institut der Freien Universität Berlin.) Berlin. 1952– . Annual.

Each volume contains a bibliography of articles and books recently published, primarily in Germany, concerning the history of central and eastern Germany, with emphasis on the modern period. The publications are divided into two parts: books, and articles and select tables of contents of recent periodicals. Each part contains a general section, followed by sections devoted to Berlin, Brandenburg, Mecklenburg and Pomerania, West and East Prussia, Saxony-Anhalt (province), Thuringia, Saxony (region), the Wends, Silesia, and border districts. Signed critical reviews (up to 2,500 words) for books. Occasional brief descriptive annotations for articles. Author index (for books only). Bibliography began in 1959.

Examined: vols. 13–14 (1965), bibliography for 1962–64, *ca.* 500 books, *ca.* 1,000 articles, *ca.* 400 serials indexed.

61. Jahrbuch für Geschichte und Kunst des Mittelrheins und seiner Nachbargebiete. (Verein für Geschichte und Kunst des Mittelrheins.) Neuwied am Rhein. 1949–   (publ. 1950–   ). Biennial.

Each double volume contains the "Bibliographie zur Landes- und Ortsgeschichte des Mittelrheins," which includes articles and books published in Europe and North America during a given period concerning the history, art, and culture of the middle Rhineland and vicinity. The publications are classified by topic within eleven major sections: *Allgemeines, Hilfswissenschaften, Geschichte und Landeskunde, Kirchengeschichte, Recht und Verwaltung, Kriegs- und Wehrwesen, Wirtschafts- und Sozialgeschichte, Gesundheitswesen, Geistes- und Kulturgeschichte, Volkskunde, Familien- und Personengeschichte.* The bibliography began in 1956–57.

Examined: vol. 17 (1965, publ. 1966), bibliography for 1960, 954 items.

*62. Jahresberichte für deutsche Geschichte. (Abteilung Bibliographie und Documentation des Instituts für Geschichte, Deutsche Akademie der Wissenschaften zu Berlin.) Berlin. 1925–   (publ. 1927–   ). Biennial.

Continues **Jahresberichte der deutschen Geschichte.** Breslau. 1918–24 (publ. 1920–26).

Each biennial volume comprises an extensive bibliography of articles and books published during a given period in Europe and North America concerning the history of the German peoples and states from antiquity until 1945. The publications are extensively classified under two major headings: *Bibliographie und Hilfswissenschaften*, subdivided by topic; and *Geschichtswissenschaft, Quellen und Darstellungen*, subdivided by topic and historical period. Occasional brief descriptive annotations. Reviews are noted. Extensive author and subject indexes. Examined: ser. 2, vols. 13–14 (1961–62, publ. 1966), bibliography for 1961–62, 10,445 items, *ca.* 1,000 serials indexed.

63. Kurtrierisches Jahrbuch. (Stadtbibliothek Trier. Gesellschaft für nützliche Forschungen.) Trier. 1961– . Annual.

Each volume contains the "Trevirensien-Bibliographie," a bibliography of articles and books published in Europe and North America during a given year concerning all aspects, historical and contemporary, of the region of Trier. The publications are classified by general subject, e.g. theology and church, history, intellectual history, law, economy, natural history, family history, and biography; each is subdivided by topic. A portion of the last heading normally is devoted to Nicholas of Cusa. Occasional brief descriptive annotations. Examined: vol. 6 (1966), bibliography for 1965, *ca.* 500 items.

64. Pfälzische Bibliographie (einschliesslich Saarschrifttum). (Pfälzische Gesellschaft zur Förderung der Wissenschaften.) Speyer. 1951– (publ. 1952–). Irregular.
    Continues **Pfälzische Bibliographie.** D. Häberle, ed. Vols. 1–4, Heidelberg, 1908–19; vols. 5–6 (Pfälzische Gesellschaft zur Förderung der Wissenschaften), Speyer, 1927–28.

Each volume comprises a bibliography of articles and books published during a given period, principally in Germany, concerning the history and culture of the Palatinate and the Saarland from antiquity to the present. Classified by topic. Reviews are noted. Author and subject index. Examined: 1958–59 (publ. 1965), bibliography for 1958–59, 4,963 items.

65. Saarländische Bibliographie. (Kommission für saarländische Landesgeschichte und Volksforschung.) Saarbrücken. 1961– (publ. 1964–). Biennial.

An extensive bibliography of articles and books recently published, primarily in Germany, concerning all aspects, historical and contemporary, of the Saarland. The publications are classified by topic under twelve major headings: *Allgemeines; Landeskunde; Bevölkerung, Siedlung, Volkskunde; Geschichte; Kirche und Religion; Recht und Verwaltung; Wirtschaft; Sozial- und Gesundheitswesen; Sport; Geistiges und kulturelles Leben; Ortsbeschreibung und Ortsgeschichte; Personen- und Familiengeschichte, Biographien.* Reviews are occasionally noted. Indexes of authors and of serials and series.
  Examined: vol. 2 (1963–64, publ. 1966), bibliography for 1963–64, 3,738 items.

66. Sächsische Bibliographie. (Sächsische Landesbibliothek.) Dresden. 1961– (publ. 1962–). Annual.
  Continues **Bibliographie der sächsischen Geschichte.** R. Bemmann and J. Jatzwauk, eds. 3 vols. Leipzig and Berlin. 1918–32.

Each issue comprises an extensive bibliography of articles and books published in Germany during a given year concerning all aspects of Saxony, historical and contemporary. The publications are classified by topic within major sections, e.g. *Natur, Geschichte, Verwaltung und Recht, Kultur,* and *Kirche.* One major section, *Orte,* is devoted to individual cities (Dresden, Freiburg, Leipzig, etc.). Occasional brief descriptive annotations. Author and subject indexes.
  Examined: 1965 (publ. 1966), bibliography for 1961–64, 2,062 items.

67. Württembergische Geschichtsliteratur. (Kommission für geschichtliche Landeskunde in Baden-Württemberg. Württembergische Geschichts- und Altertumsverein.) Stuttgart. 1946– (publ. 1952–). Annual.
  Supplement to **Zeitschrift für württembergische Landesgeschichte.** (Kommission für geschichtliche Landeskunde in Baden-Württemberg. Württembergische Geschichts- und Altertumsverein.) Stuttgart.

Continues **Bibliographie der württembergischen Geschichte.** Founded by Wilhelm Heyd. (Württembergische Kommission für Landesgeschichte.) 8 vols. Stuttgart. 1895–1945 (publ. 1895–1956).

Each volume comprises a bibliography of articles and books published during a given year in Europe and North America concerning the history of Württemberg. Classified by topic, geographic region, and individual or family under three headings: *Allgemeine Landesgeschichte, Ortsgeschichte,* and *Biographisches und Familiengeschichte.* The bibliography is cumulated irregularly as a continuation of Heyd.

Examined: 1962 (publ. 1964), bibliography for 1962, *ca.* 1,500 items.

68. Zeitschrift des Vereins für hessische Geschichte und Landeskunde. (Verein für hessische Geschichte und Landeskunde.) Kassel. 1837– . Annual.

Every second volume normally contains a bibliography of articles and books published during a given period, primarily in Germany, concerning the former Electorate of Hesse from antiquity to the present. The publications are classified by topic within fifteen major sections, e.g. *Landeskunde, Kirchengeschichte, Kunst.* The bibliography began in 1903.

Examined: vol. 74 (1963, publ. 1964), bibliography for 1962, 611 items.

See also:
20. **Zeitschrift für Geschichtswissenschaft**
88. **Zeitschrift für Ostforschung**
103. **Archivalische Zeitschrift**
121. **Ausgrabungen und Funde**
122. **Bayerische Vorgeschichtsblätter**
130. **Kölner Domblatt**
135. **Schrifttum zur deutschen Kunst**
163. **Hansische Geschichtsblätter**
242. **Bibliographie der deutschen Literaturwissenschaft**
244. **Germanistik**
247. **Jahresbericht für deutsche Sprache und Literatur**

F. Italy

69. Atti della Società ligure di storia patria. (Società ligure di storia patria.) Genova. 1858– . Semiannual.

The second number of each annual volume contains a bibliography of articles and books recently published, primarily in Italy, concerning Liguria from antiquity to the present. The publications are arranged by chronological period including sections on general and auxiliary studies. Signed descriptive annotations (up to 400 words). The bibliography began in 1963.
Examined: vol. 3 (1963), bibliography for 1961–62, *ca.* 175 items.

70. Bibliografia romana. (Istituto di studi romani.) Roma. 1948– (publ. 1949–). Annual.
Continues **Saggio di bibliografia romana** for 1945–48, reprinted from **Strenna dei romanisti:** Natale di Roma. Roma. 1946–48. And "Largo dei librari: Bibliografia romana tra due natali di Roma," published 1943–45 in **Strenna dei romanisti.**

An extensive bibliography of articles and books published during a given year, principally in Europe and North America, concerning the city of Rome from antiquity to the present, with emphasis on the modern period. Publications are classified by topic. Frequent descriptive annotations (up to 1,500 words). Reviews are noted. Author and subject indexes.
Examined: vol. 11 (1955, publ. 1963), bibliography for 1955, *ca.* 5,000 items, *ca.* 450 serials indexed.

71. Italian Studies. (Society for Italian Studies.) Cambridge. 1937– . Annual.

Each volume contains a bibliography of articles and books published during the previous year, primarily in Great Britain, concerning the history and culture of Italy from the Middle Ages through the modern period. Classified by topic: *Art and Architecture; History and Philosophy; Language; Literature and Criticism; Miscellaneous; Music; Travel, Description and Geography; Bibliography.* Reviews are noted.
Examined: vol. 20 (1965), bibliography for 1964, *ca.* 350 items.

See also:
3. **Bibliografia storica nazionale**
108. **Quellen und Forschungen aus italienischen Archiven und Bibliotheken**
125. **Commentari**
159. **Rivista di storia della chiesa in Italia**
208. **Bibliografia filosofica italiana**
253. **L'Alighieri**
261. **La rassegna della letteratura italiana**

G. Scandinavia

72. Árbók. (Landsbokasafn Íslands.) Reykjavík. 1944– . (publ. 1945–). Annual.

Each annual volume contains a bibliography of books recently published, primarily in Iceland but also in Europe and North America, concerning the historical and contemporary culture of Iceland. The bibliography is divided into two sections: *Íslenzk Rit* (books published in Iceland in Icelandic, with a subject index and a separate section devoted to items omitted from previous bibliographies) and *Rit á erlendum Tungum* (publications, including select articles, concerning Iceland in non-Icelandic languages). The publications in both sections are arranged alphabetically by author. Frequent cross-references.

Examined: vol. 22 (1965, publ. 1966), bibliography for 1964, *ca.* 1,200 items.

73. Bibliografi til norges historie. (Norske historiske forening.) Oslo. 1916– (publ. 1927–). Biennial.

Published as a separately paginated supplement in **Historisk tidsskrift.** (Norske historiske forening.) Oslo.

An extensive bibliography of articles and books published during a given two-year period in Europe and North America concerning Norwegian history from antiquity to the present. Publications are classified by topic: bibliography, national history, local history, former Norwegian possessions (Iceland, Faeroe Islands, etc.), biography, cultural history and folklore, art, literature, religion and church, justice and social conditions, commerce and economy. Decennial author and subject index.

Examined: 1962–63 (publ. 1965), bibliography for 1962–63, 1,745 items.

74. Excerpta historica Nordica. (International Committee of Historical Sciences.) København. 1955– . Biennial.

Each volume comprises a bibliography of articles and books published in the Scandinavian countries during a given two-year period concerning world and especially Scandinavian history. The publications are classified in four sections: *Denmark, Finland, Norway,* and *Sweden.* Each section contains a brief bibliographic survey of historical work in that country and a list of its publications arranged chronologically by contents from antiquity to the present. Many items are accompanied by English or German summaries (up to 5,000 words). Reviews are occasionally noted. Author index.

Examined: vol. 4 (1959–60, publ. 1965), bibliography for 1959–60, *ca.* 250 items.

75. Svensk historisk bibliografi. (Svenska historiska föreningen.) Stockholm. 1880– (publ. 1881–). Annual.
  Supplement to **Historisk tidskrift.** (Svenska historiska föreningen.) Stockholm.
  Cumulated and reprinted as **Svensk historisk bibliografi.** K. Setterwall, ed. (Svenska historiska föreningen.) Stockholm and Uppsala. 1875–1900 (publ. 1907), 1901–20 (publ. 1923), 1921–35 (publ. 1956).
  Continues **Svensk historisk bibliografi, 1775–1874.** K. Setterwall, ed. (Svenska historiska föreningen.) Uppsala. 1937.

Each volume comprises an extensive bibliography of articles and books published during a given year in Europe and North America concerning the history of Sweden and her peoples from antiquity to the present. Publications are classified by topic: bibliography, political history, biography, heraldry and numismatics, law, economic and social history, church history, history of education, military history, local history, cultural history, Finland, Swedes abroad, book reviews. Reviews are noted. Author index.

Examined: 1963 (publ. 1966), bibliography for 1963, 1,768 items.

See also:
163. **Hansische Geschichtsblätter**
243. **Bibliography of Old Norse-Icelandic Studies**
246. **Íslenzk tunga**
248. **Scandinavian Studies**
249. **Svensk litteraturhistorisk bibliografi**
281. **Lychnos**

H. Slavic Countries, Hungary, and Romania

76. **Acta historica:** Revue de l'Académie des sciences de Hongrie. (Magyar Tudományos Akadémia.) Budapest. 1951–
Semiannual.

Each issue contains a bibliography of articles and books recently published in Hungary pertaining to world and especially Hungarian history. Classified by general topic and chronological period. Titles in Hungarian, French, and Russian. Frequent descriptive annotations (up to 100 words) in French. Reviews in Hungarian journals are noted. The bibliography began in 1958.
Examined: vol. 10 (1964), bibliography for 1961–62, *ca.* 500 items.

77. **The American Bibliography of Russian and East European Studies.** (Russian and East European Institute, Indiana University.) Bloomington, Indiana. 1956–   (publ. 1957–   ). Annual.
Entitled **The American Bibliography of Slavic and East European Studies in Language, Literature, Folklore, and Pedagogy,** 1956.

Each volume comprises an extensive bibliography of articles and books published in English during a given year throughout the world (excepting the Soviet Union and the eastern European countries) concerning Russia and eastern Europe up to the present. The bibliography is classified by topic or geographic area under the following headings: *General; Anthropology and Archaeology; Geography; History; International Relations; Public Affairs, Law and Government; Economics; Science; Sociology; Philosophy, Ideology and Religion; Education; Linguistics; Lit-*

erature and the Arts; Folklore. The focus of the bibliography is on the modern period. Translations from Russian to English are excluded. Significant reviews are listed by reviewer. Biobibliographic (persons mentioned in titles) and author indexes. Coverage expanded to include both the humanities and the social sciences after the first volume.
Examined: 1964 (publ. 1966), bibliography for 1964, 2,260 items, *ca.* 400 serials indexed.

78. Bibliografia historii polskiej. (Instytut Historii, Polska Akademia Nauk.) Wrocław, Warszawa, Kraków. 1948–   (publ. 1952–   ). Annual.

An extensive bibliography of articles and books published during a given year in Poland concerning history and historiography in general, or published in Europe and North America concerning Polish history from its beginnings to the present. Extensively classified by topic and historical period under three major headings: general, auxiliary sciences, Polish history. Occasional descriptive annotations (up to 300 words). Reviews are noted. Author and subject index. Additional volumes are planned to cover previous years.
Examined: 1963 (publ. 1965), bibliography for 1963, 4,060 items.

79. Bibliografie československé historie. (Československá akademie věd.) Praha. 1955–   (publ. 1957–   ). Annual.
Continues **Bibliografie české historie.** (Historický klub.) Praha. 1904–41 (publ. 1905–51). Annual. Published 1905–38 as a supplement to **Český časopis historický.** (Historický klub.) Praha.

Each annual volume comprises an extensive bibliography of articles and books published during a given year in Czechoslovakia concerning history in general, or published in Europe and North America concerning Czechoslovakian history from its beginnings to the present. The publications on Czechoslovakian history are classified by chronological period, including a section on the Hussite movement. A separate section is devoted to auxiliary sciences including archaeology, paleography, heraldry, and bibliography. The Czechoslovakian publications on history in general are classified by chronological period and by individual country. Book reviews are noted. Previous to the volume for 1961, this work contained extensive bibliographies on the history of Czechoslovakian agriculture, technology, music, printing, and similar topics. Beginning with the volume for 1961, book reviews for items in previous bibliographies are listed in two sections, Czechoslovakian and world history. Indexes of authors and anonymous works.

Examined: 1961 (publ. 1965), bibliography for 1961, 9,264 items, *ca.* 500 serials indexed.

80. Istorijski glasnik [Historical Herald]. (Društvo istoričara, Narodne Republike Srbije.) Beograd. 1948– . Semiannual.

One issue of each annual volume normally contains a bibliography of articles and books published during the previous year, principally in Yugoslavia, concerning the history of that country from antiquity to the present. Classified by topic and historical period.

Examined: 1965, bibliography for 1964, *ca.* 850 items.

81. Revue des études slaves. (Institut d'études slaves.) Paris. 1921– . Annual.

Each volume normally contains a series of signed bibliographic essays discussing articles and books recently published in Europe and North America concerning Slavic culture and history from their origins to the present. Each essay covers a specific topic, such as economics, linguistics, or folklore. The essays are normally arranged under the following headings: *Généralités, Russe, Ukrainien, Blanc-Russe, Tchèque, Slovaque, Polonais, Poméranien, Polabe, Sorabe, Serbo-Croate, Slovène, Macédonien, Bulgare.*

Examined: vol. 43 (1964), bibliography for 1962–63, 57 essays.

82. Revue des études sud-est européennes. (Institut d'études sud-est européennes, Académie de la République Populaire Roumaine.) Bucureşti. 1963– . Semiannual.

Each issue contains a bibliography of articles and books recently published throughout Europe concerning the history of southeastern Europe from the Byzantine through the early modern period. The publications are normally grouped by general subject. Initialed descriptive annotations (up to 250 words). Examined: vol. 2 (1964), bibliography for 1962–63, 123 items.

83. Revue roumaine d'histoire. (Académie de la République Socialiste de Roumanie.) Bucureşti. 1962–   . Six issues yearly.

Two issues of each annual volume normally contain a bibliography of articles and books published in Romania during a given year concerning primarily Romanian history from the earliest times through the present. The publications are classified by chronological period and general topic, e.g. *Histoire ancienne, Histoire du Moyen Age, Histoire de la culture et de l'art, Histoire universelle, Archives, méthodologie, instruments de travail.* French translations are given for Romanian titles. Bibliography began in 1964.
Examined; vol. 4 (1965), bibliography for 1963, 374 items.

84. Sobótka: Śląski kwartalnik historyczny [Bonfire: Silesian Historical Quarterly]. (Wrocławskie Towarzystwo Miłośników Historii.) Wrocław. 1946–   . Semiannual.

Each annual volume normally contains a bibliography of articles and books published during the previous year, principally in Poland, concerning various aspects of Silesian history, from its beginnings to the present. The publications are classified by topic. Reviews are noted. Bibliography began in 1960.
Examined: vol. 19 (1964), bibliography for 1963, 1,392 items.

85. Studia historica Slovaca. (Historický ústav, Slovenská akadémia vied.) Bratislava. 1963–   . Annual.

Every second volume contains a review essay surveying articles and books published during a given two-year period, primarily in Czechoslovakia, concerning all aspects of Slovakian history and culture up to the present. The essay, in paragraph form, is organized by general subject and historical period, including *L'époque féodale.*

Examined: vol. 3 (1965), bibliography for 1963–64, 231 items.

86. Südosteuropa-Bibliographie. (Südost-Institut.) München. 1945– (publ. 1956–). Irregular.

Each volume comprises an extensive bibliography of articles and books published throughout the world during a given five-year period concerning the peoples of Yugoslavia, Hungary, Albania, Bulgaria, Romania, and Slovakia. The bibliography for each of these areas is separately edited, and each is subdivided into nine sections: *Allgemeines, Das Land, Bevölkerung, Geschichte und Politik, Sprache und Literatur, Religion und Kirche, Staat und Recht, Wirtschaft und Sozialwesen, Geistiges und kulturelles Leben.* Occasional brief descriptive annotations. Author index.

Examined: vol. 2 (1951–55, publ. 1960–62), bibliography for 1951–55, 10,215 items.

87. Századok [Centuries]. (Magyar Történelmi Társulat.) Budapest. 1867– . Quarterly.

Two issues of each annual volume contain a bibliography of articles and books recently published, primarily in Hungary and by Hungarians, concerning Hungarian and world history from antiquity to the present. The publications are classified by topic and chronological period in two sections: Hungarian history and general history. Reviews are noted. Bibliography began in 1954.

Examined: vol. 98 (1964), bibliography for 1963, *ca.* 1,500 items.

88. Zeitschrift für Ostforschung: Länder und Völker im östlichen Mitteleuropa. (Johann Gottfried Herder-Forschungsrat.) Marburg. 1952– . Quarterly.

Each issue contains one or more bibliographies of articles and books published during a given period, primarily in Germany and eastern Europe, concerning a particular region of eastern Central Europe. These bibliographies, each appearing annually or biennially, are "Baltische Bibliographie," "Schrifttum über Estland und Lettland in Auswahl," "Schrifttum über Ostbrandenburg und dessen Grenzgebiete," "Schrifttum zur Ge-

schichte von Ost- und Westpreussen," "Schrifttum über das Posener Land," "Schrifttum über Schlesien," "Auswahlbibliographie
zur Geschichte und Landeskunde der Sudetenländer." Each
is classified by topic, e.g. ecclesiastical, economic, intellectual,
legal, political, or social history. Brief descriptive annotations
in German for Slavic titles. The Herder-Forschungsrat also publishes a series **Wissenschaftliche Beiträge zur Geschichte und
Landeskunde Ost-Mitteleuropas** which includes several monographic bibliographies covering these same regions and being es-
sentially expansions of the smaller bibliographies: **Schlesische
Bibliographie,** H. Rister, ed.; **Schrifttum über Polen mit besonder
Berücksichtigung des Posener Landes,** H. Rister, ed.; **Bibliographie der Geschichte von Ost- und Westpreussen,** E. Wermke,
ed.; **Geschichtliche und landeskundliche Literatur Pommerns,**
H.-U. Raspe and H. Rister, eds.; **Sudetendeutsche Bibliographie,**
J. Hemmerle, ed.

Examined: vol. 14 (1965), bibliographies for 1962–64, 1,086
items.

See also:
57. **Jahrbuch der Albertus-Universität zu Königsberg, Preussen**
60. **Jahrbuch für die Geschichte Mittel- und Ostdeutschlands**
93. **Byzantinoslavica**
113. **Wiadomości numizmatyczne**
121. **Ausgrabungen und Funde**
145. **Ostkirchliche Studien**
161. **Bibliographia historiae rerum rusticarum internationalis**
163. **Hansische Geschichtsblätter**
   Section IX-E, Slavic Languages

I. Spain and Portugal

89. **Cuadernos de estudios gallegos.** (Instituto Padre Sarmiento
   de estudios gallegos.) Santiago de Compostela. 1944– .
   Three issues yearly.

The last number of each annual volume normally contains the
"Bibliografía de Galicia," which includes articles and books recently published, principally in Spain and Portugal, concerning
the history and culture of the region of Galicia in northwestern

42   SERIAL BIBLIOGRAPHIES

Spain. Classified by subject. The bibliography lists publications concerning such topics as pilgrimages to St. James of Compostela, local monasteries and churches, folklore, medieval literature, and the Galician Ibero-romance dialect. Occasional brief descriptive annotations. Author index.
Examined: vol. 20 (1965), bibliography for 1963–65, 528 items.

90. Índice histórico español. (Centro de estudios históricos internacionales, Universidad de Barcelona.) Barcelona. 1953– . Three issues yearly.

Each issue comprises an extensive bibliography of articles and books recently published throughout the world concerning Spanish and Spanish American history and civilization from antiquity to the present. Classified by topic, historical period, and geographic region. Initialed descriptive annotations (up to 150 words.). Reviews are noted. Annual author and subject index published separately.
Examined: vol. 9 (1963, publ. 1966), bibliography for 1962–63, 4,142 items.

See also:
    217. Estudios eclesiásticos
    257. Bulletin hispanique
    260. Nueva revista de filología hispánica
    262. Revista de filología española

III. Byzantine, Islamic, and Judaic Studies

A. Byzantium

91. Bulletin analytique de bibliographie hellénique. (Institut français d'Athènes.) Athenai. 1946–   (publ. 1947–   ). Annual.

Each volume comprises an extensive bibliography in two parts concerning all aspects of current scholarly publication in Greece. The first part contains books published during a given year, primarily in Greece. These publications are classified by topic within five major divisions: *Littérature, Sciences, Sciences humaines, Livres scholaires, Traductions.* Titles are given in Greek and in French translation. Descriptive annotations (up to 150 words). The second part contains an extensive list of select tables of contents of primarily Greek journals, arranged by general subject: *Art et littérature, Mélanges, Sciences, Sciences humaines.* Titles of articles normally are given in French. Index of names for both parts. Volumes are planned for 1940–45.

Examined: vol. 22 (1961, publ. 1964), bibliography for 1961, 2,320 books, 470 journals.

*92. Byzantinische Zeitschrift. München. 1892– . Semiannual.

Each issue contains an extensive bibliography of articles and books recently published, principally in Europe and North America, concerning Byzantine history (325 to 1453). The publications are classified by topic within twelve major sections: *Literatur und Sagen; Handschriften- und Bücherkunde, Urkunden, Gelehrtengeschichte; Sprache, Metrik und Musik; Theologie; Geschichte; Geographie, Topographie, Ethnographie; Kunstgeschichte; Numismatik, Sigillographie, Heraldik; Epigraphik; Byzantinisches Recht; Fachwissenschaften; Mitteilungen.* Frequent descriptive annotations (up to 500 words). Reviews are noted. Annual author index.

Examined: vol. 57 (1964), bibliography for 1963–64, *ca.* 2,250 items.

*93. Byzantinoslavica: Revue internationale des études byzantines. Praha. 1929– . Semiannual.

Each number contains an extensive bibliography of articles and books recently published in Europe (especially the Slavic countries) and North America concerning Byzantine history, with some emphasis on Byzantino-Slavic relations, from the Roman-Christian period to the fall of Trebizond (1461). Classified by topic within ten major sections: *Byzantinologie; Langues; Belles-lettres et folklore, métrique; Sources historiques et monographiques; Histoire; Sciences auxiliaires; Philosophie et théologie; Géographie et topographie, Ethnographie; Art byzantin, musique; Relations byzantinoslaves, relations de Byzance avec d'autres pays.* Frequent initialed descriptive annotations (up to 600 words). Reviews are noted. Annual author index. Bibliography began in 1931.

Examined: vol. 25 (1964), bibliography for 1961–63, *ca.* 2,000 items.

94. Byzantion: Revue internationale des études byzantines. (Société belge d'études byzantines.) Bruxelles. 1924– . Semiannual.

Each issue contains a list of articles and books recently published in Europe, the Slavic countries, and North America concerning all aspects of Byzantine history and culture. The pub-

lications are listed alphabetically by author. Initialed descriptive annotations (up to 250 words). Reviews are occasionally noted. Bibliography began in 1962.
Examined: vol. 35 (1965), bibliography for 1963–65, *ca.* 225 items.

95. Epeteris tês Hetaireias byzantinon spoudon. Annuaire de l'Association d'études byzantines. (Hetaireia byzantinon spoudon.) Athenai. 1924– . Annual.

Each volume contains a bibliography of articles and books recently published in Greece, western Europe, and North America concerning the political, cultural, and ecclesiastical history of Byzantium. The publications are classified by general topic, including philology, theology, political history, ecclesiastical history, drama, and law.
Examined: vol. 33 (1964), bibliography for 1963–64, *ca.* 400 items.

96. Parnassos: Periodikon syggramma kata trimenian ekdidomenon. (Philologikos syllogos parnassos.) Athenai. 1877– . Quarterly.

The fourth issue of each annual volume contains the "Bibliographikon deltion neoellenikes philologias," a bibliography of articles and books published during a given year, primarily in Greece, concerning various aspects of the cultural history of Greece. One section, *Demodes mesaionike logotechnia,* is devoted to Byzantine philology and literature. Another section, *Demode asmata, mnemeia laikou logou,* is devoted to folklore. Index of names. Bibliography began in 1959.
Examined: ser. 2, vol. 4 (1962), bibliography for 1961, 481 items.

See also:

B. Islam

*97. Abstracta Islamica. Paris. 1927–   . Annual.
Published as a separately paginated supplement in **Revue des études islamiques.** Paris.

An extensive bibliography of articles and books recently published throughout the world concerning Islamic history and culture from their origins to the present. The publications are classified by topic, historical period, and geographic region within five major sections: *Histoire politique et sociale; Culture islamique classique; Arts, techniques et archéologie; Réformisme, modernisme et nationalisme dans l'Islam contemporain; Bibliographie et divers.* Frequent initialed descriptive or critical annotations (up to 200 words). Reviews are noted. Author index.
Examined: vol. 19 (1965), bibliography for 1963–64, 1,499 items; in **Revue des études islamiques,** vol. 33 (1965).

*98. Index Islamicus: A Catalogue of Articles on Islamic Subjects in Periodicals and Other Collective Publications. J. D. Pearson, ed. Cambridge. 1906–   (publ. 1958–   ). Quinquennial.

An extensive bibliography of articles published during a given five-year period throughout the world concerning all aspects of Islamic civilization in North Africa, the Middle East, Central Asia, India, and Pakistan. The publications are classified by subject, historical period, and country or geographic region. Sections are devoted to Arabic sciences and the transmission of Greek thought to the West, Muslim travelers, numismatics, the Califate, the crusades and the Latin kingdoms, Muslims in Europe, the Ottoman and Seljuk Turks, and the Mongols. Titles in nonroman alphabets are transliterated and translated. Author index. The first volume covered the years 1906–55; a revised second edition was published in 1961.
Examined: 1956–60 (publ. 1962), bibliography for 1956–60, 7,296 items, *ca.* 900 serials and collective works indexed.

99. The Middle East Journal. (Middle East Institute.) Washington, D.C. 1947–   . Quarterly.

Each issue normally contains a bibliography of articles recently published in Europe, North America, and the Middle East concerning the history of the Near and Middle East from the advent of Islam to the present. Publications are classified by topic. Book reviews are listed separately by author being reviewed.

Examined: vol. 21 (1967), bibliography for 1966–67, 1,698 items, *ca.* 120 serials indexed.

See also:
10. International Bibliography of Historical Sciences
21. Annual Bibliography of Oriental Studies
23. Orientalistische Literaturzeitung
139. International Bibliography of the History of Religions
140. Répertoire général de sciences religieuses
214. Bulletin signalétique 19: Philosophie, sciences religieuses

C. Judaic Studies

100. **Kirjath Sepher** [City of the Book]. (Jewish National and University Library.) Jerusalem. 1924– . Quarterly.

Each issue contains a bibliography of articles and books recently published throughout the world concerning the history of the Jewish people, with emphasis on the present. Publications are classified in three sections: books published in Israel, books published elsewhere (both subdivided by topic), and periodical literature (arranged by serial title). Brief descriptive annotations. Most items are in Hebrew. Annual indexes of names (including journal titles).

Examined: vol. 42 (1966–67), bibliography for 1965–66, 4,477 items.

101. **Sefarad:** Revista del Instituto Arias Montano de estudios hebraicos y Oriente Próximo. (Instituto Arias Montano.) Madrid and Barcelona. 1941– . Semiannual.

Each issue contains a list of select tables of contents for journals recently published throughout the world in the field of Near Eastern history from antiquity to the present, with particular emphasis upon the earlier periods and upon Jewish civilization. The tables of contents are listed alphabetically by journal

title. Frequent initialed descriptive or critical annotations (up to 100 words).
   Examined: vol. 26 (1966), bibliography for 1965–66, *ca.* 100 journals listed.

102. Year Book. (Leo Baeck Institute.) London, Jerusalem, New York. 1956– . Annual.

Each issue contains "Post-War Publications on German Jewry," a bibliography of articles and books published during a given year in Europe and North America concerning all aspects of the history and culture of the Jews in Germany and Central Europe. While the bibliography deals primarily with the modern period, the first section, *History,* includes publications concerning the Jews in Germany, Austria, and Czechoslovakia during the Middle Ages. Frequent brief descriptive annotations. Author and subject index.
   Examined: vol. 10 (1965), bibliography for 1964, 675 items.

See also:
   10. International Bibliography of Historical Sciences
   23. Orientalistische Literaturzeitung
   134. Rivista di archeologia cristiana
   139. International Bibliography of the History of Religions
   140. Répertoire général de sciences religieuses
   196. Internationale Zeitschriftenschau für Bibelwissenschaft und Grenzgebiete
   214. Bulletin signalétique 19: Philosophie, sciences religieuses

PART TWO

PART TWO

IV. Archival and Auxiliary Studies

A. Archives and Manuscripts

103. Archivalische Zeitschrift. (Bayerisches Hauptstaatsarchiv, München.) Köln and Graz. 1876– . Annual.

Each annual volume contains a bibliography of articles and books recently published, principally in the German and Slavic languages, concerning primarily East and West German archives, but also including Bohemian, Slovakian, Austrian, and Swiss archives and their contents. Classified by topic and by political region. The journal also contains an annotated (up to 150 words) list of tables of contents of European and North American journals dealing with archives.

Examined: vol. 60 (1964), bibliography for 1962–63, *ca.* 225 items, *ca.* 50 journals.

104. Der Archivar: Mitteilungsblatt für deutsches Archivwesen. (Verein deutscher Archivare.) Siegburg. 1947– . Quarterly.

Three issues in each two-year period normally contain the "Bibliographie zum Archivwesen," which includes articles and books published during a given period, primarily in Europe, concerning archives and their contents in Germany and neighboring countries. The publications are classified by country or geographic region; international archives; archives in general (primarily in Germany); individual archives in the Federal Republic, Berlin, the Democratic Republic, and in former German territory; biographical notices of German archivists; and archives in Austria, Switzerland, Belgium, Netherlands, Luxembourg, Denmark, Sweden, Poland. Each area is subdivided by topic. The first issue of the bibliography covers 1945–46.

Examined: vol. 19 (1966), bibliography for 1963–64, 1,552 items.

105. Bibliografia dell'Archivio Vaticano. (Commissione internazionale per la bibliografia dell'Archivio Vaticano.) Città del Vaticano. 1962– . Irregular.

This bibliography is intended to cover all significant articles and books published concerning Vatican archival materials since Cardinal Baronius' *Annales ecclesiastici* (1588). The first section, *Autori e opere*, lists by author publications citing Vatican documents and editions and translations of Vatican documents. The second, *Fondi e documenti*, is a comprehensive index to these publications arranged by individual Vatican manuscript. The **Bibliografia** is being published in reverse order, working back from the present; e.g. vol. 1 contains works published since 1930, vols. 2 and 3, works published since 1920. Current publications and works omitted in previous volumes are included in each volume. Index of archival signatures.

Examined: vol. 4 (1966), bibliography since 1881, 682 items.

106. Bibliographie analytique internationale des publications relatives à l'archivistique et aux archives. (Conseil international des archives.) Paris. 1958– (publ. 1964–). Irregular.

Supplement to **Archivum:** Revue internationale des archives. (Conseil international des archives.) Paris.

Continues "Bibliographie analytique internationale des publications relatives à l'archivistique et aux archives," published in **Archivum,** 1952–59.

An extensive bibliography of articles and books published throughout the world during a given period concerning archival sciences, e.g. special archives, archival administration, classification, conservation, auxiliary sciences, cartography, and notices concerning the profession and its members. Part I contains publications in the broad area of archival science which are alphabetically arranged within twenty-three subjects, including *Histoire des archives* and *Sciences complémentaires de l'archivistique* (paleography, diplomatics, sigillography, paper). Part II contains publications concerning individual local and national archives which are classified by country and subdivided by type of archive (central, provincial, municipal, ecclesiastical, business, private, etc.). Frequent brief descriptive annotations. Indexes of places and subjects.

Examined: no. 1 (1958–59, publ. 1964), bibliography for 1958–59, 2,885 items.

107. Bullettino dell' "Archivio paleografico italiano": Rivista italiana di paleografia, diplomatica e scienze ausiliarie della storia. (Istituto di paleografia, Università di Roma.) Roma. 1908– . Biennial.

Each volume contains a brief annotated bibliography ("Schede bibliografiche") of articles and books recently published, primarily in Europe and North America, concerning Latin and vernacular paleography, diplomatics, and calligraphy. The bibliography begins with a short bibliographic essay on a given topic; following this the publications are listed at random. Each item is accompanied by an initialed descriptive or critical annotation (up to 1,000 words). In previous issues, the bibliography took the form of a review article by one author. The journal also contains a number of signed critical reviews of current books. Bibliography began in 1955.

Examined: ser. 3, vols. 2–3 (1963–64), bibliography for 1961–63, 31 annotations.

108. Quellen und Forschungen aus italienischen Archiven und Bibliotheken. (Deutsches historisches Institut im Rom.) Tübingen. 1897– . Annual.

Each volume contains a bibliography of articles and books recently published in Europe and North America which are based wholly or in part on materials in Italian ecclesiastical or secular archives and libraries. The studies range from the early Middle Ages to the twentieth century and frequently pertain to some aspect of institutional or intellectual history. They are arranged by topic, historical period, or geographic area. Initialed descriptive annotations (up to 500 words). Author index.

Examined: vol. 45 (1965), bibliography for 1964–65, *ca.* 100 items.

*109. Scriptorium: Revue internationale des études relatives aux manuscrits. International Review of Manuscript Studies. Bruxelles. 1946–   . Semiannual.

Each number contains the "Bulletin codicologique," a bibliography of articles and books recently published, principally in Europe and North America, concerning the study of text and illuminated manuscripts. Publications are arranged alphabetically by author. Initialed descriptive or critical annotations (up to 750 words). An elaborate subject index including manuscripts cited appears in the last number of each annual volume. The bibliography assumed its present form in 1959. Previous to this, each bibliography was devoted to the publications of a single country or region pertaining to codicology.

Examined: vol. 19 (1965), bibliography for 1963–64, 900 items.

See also:
    7. **Deutsches Archiv für Erforschung des Mittelalters**
    141. **Revue d'histoire ecclésiastique: Bibliographie**
    143. **Aegyptus**

B. Heraldry

110. Revue française d'héraldique et de sigillographie. (Société française d'héraldique et de sigillographie.) Paris. 1938–   . Annual.

Each number contains a brief bibliography of articles and books recently published, primarily in Europe and North America, concerning heraldry, sigillography, and to a limited degree genealogy from the Middle Ages to the present. The publications are classified by country. Occasional descriptive annotations (up to 125 words.) Bibliography assumed its present form in 1955. Examined: vol. 18 (1964), bibliography for 1963, *ca.* 75 items.

See also:
   7. Deutsches Archiv für Erforschung des Mittelalters
   141. Revue d'histoire ecclésiastique: Bibliographie

C. Numismatics

111. Hamburger Beiträge zur Numismatik. (Abteilung Münzkabinett, Museum für hamburgische Geschichte.) Hamburg. 1947– . Annual.

Each annual number contains a bibliography of articles and books recently published in Europe and North America concerning the study of the coins, seals, and money of the past and present. Publications are classified by historical period and geographic area. Signed descriptive or critical annotations (up to 1,000 words). Triennial author index.
   Examined: vol. 6 (1964–65), bibliographies for 1963–65, *ca.* 600 items.

112. Numismatic Literature. (American Numismatic Society.) New York. 1947– . Quarterly.

Each number comprises a bibliography of articles and books recently published throughout the world concerning numismatics. Publications are classified by chronological period, geographic region, or country, with additional sections devoted to medals, seals, and paper money. Descriptive annotations (up to 150 words). Book reviews are listed in a separate section by author being reviewed. Biennial author and subject indexes.
   Examined: nos. 66–69 (1964), bibliography for 1962–63, *ca.* 1,500 items.

113. Wiadomości numizmatyczne [Numismatic Announcements]. (Polskie Towarzystwo Archeologiczne.) Warszawa. 1957– . Semiannual.

The second number of each annual volume frequently contains

a bibliography of articles and books published in Poland during a given year concerning numismatics in general, or published outside Poland concerning Polish numismatics. Publications are classified by subject and chronological period, with sections on medals and heraldry. Book reviews are noted. The bibliography began in 1959.
Examined: vol. 8 (1964), bibliography for 1961, 104 items.

See also:
7. **Deutsches Archiv für Erforschung des Mittelalters**
92. **Byzantinische Zeitschrift**
114. **Annuario bibliografico di archeologia**
141. **Revue d'histoire ecclésiastique: Bibliographic**

V. Art and Archaeology

114. Annuario bibliografico di archeologia. (Biblioteca dell'Istituto nazionale d'archeologia e storia dell'arte, Roma.) Modena. 1952– (publ. 1954–). Annual.

Each volume comprises an extensive bibliography of articles and books published throughout the world during a given year concerning primarily the physical remains of the past, with emphasis on Greece and Rome. Publications are classified by topic or region within fourteen sections: *Archeologia cristiana e bizantinologia; Architettura e topografia; Arti minori e industria; Ceramica; Epigrafia; Filologia; Numismatica; Pittura e mosaico; Preistoria e protostoria; Religione, etnologia; Scavi e notizie archeologiche; Scultura; Storia; Varia.* Frequent descriptive annotations (up to 100 words). Author index.

Examined: vols. 8–9 (1959–60, publ. 1966), bibliography for 1959–60, 4,402 items, *ca.* 200 serials indexed.

115. Annuario bibliografico di storia dell'arte. (Biblioteca dell'-Istituto nazionale d'archeologia e storia dell'arte, Roma.) Modena. 1952– (publ. 1954–). Annual.

An extensive bibliography of articles and books published during a given period, principally in Europe and North America, concerning art (including architecture, armor, ceramics, numismatics, tapestries, etc.), artists, and art history throughout the world, from its beginnings to the present. Classified under three major headings: *Arte* (general works arranged by topic), *Artisti*, and *Paesi* (arranged by geographic region and subdivided by topic and medium). Descriptive annotations (up to 200 words). Index of names.

Examined: vols. 8–9 (1959–60, publ. 1966), bibliography for 1959–60, 9,791 items, *ca.* 500 serials indexed.

116. Antiquaries Journal. (Society of Antiquaries of London.) London. 1921– . Semiannual.

Each issue contains a list of monographic accessions to the society's library which concern archaeology in the British Isles, Europe, and the Near East. Publications are classified by subject. Also included is a substantial list of the select contents of journals devoted to similar interests which are published in Europe and North America.

Examined: vol. 44 (1964), accessions for 1963–64, 139 items, 147 journals.

117. Archaeological Bibliography for Great Britain & Ireland. (Council for British Archaeology.) London. 1940– (publ. 1949–). Annual.

A bibliography of articles and books published in Great Britain and Ireland during a given year concerning the archaeology of the British Isles from the earliest times to 1600. The publications are listed alphabetically by author. This list is preceded by an extensive topographical index to these publications, arranged by region, subdivided by chronological period and subject. Subject index.

Examined: 1964 (publ. 1966), bibliography for 1964, 620 items, *ca.* 350 serials indexed.

118. Archäologische Bibliographie. (Deutsches archäologisches Institut.) Berlin. 1913– (publ. 1914–). Annual.

Published as a supplement to **Jahrbuch des Deutschen archäologischen Instituts.** Berlin.

Entitled **Bibliographie zum Jahrbuch des Deutschen archäologischen Instituts,** 1913–31.
Continues bibliography in **Archäologischer Anzeiger,** supplement **(Beiblatt)** to **Jahrbuch des Archäologischen Instituts,** 1889–1912; and in **Jahrbuch des Deutschen archäologischen Instituts,** 1886–88.

An extensive bibliography of articles and books published in Europe and North America during the previous year concerning particularly pre-classical and classical archaeology, with a subsection on Byzantine and Early Christian archaeology. Classified by topic. Reviews are noted. Author index.
Examined: 1964 (publ. 1966), bibliography for 1964, 4,908 items, *ca.* 300 serials indexed; supplement to **Jahrbuch,** vol. 80 (1965, publ. 1966).

119. Arte veneta: Rivista di storia dell'arte. Venezia. 1947– . Annual.

Each volume normally contains a bibliography of articles and books published during the preceding year in Europe and North America concerning Venetian art. Classified according to major subjects: sculpture, architecture, painting, engraving, minor arts. The publications of various museums and galleries are also included. Reviews are noted.
Examined: vol. 19 (1965), bibliography for 1964, *ca.* 600 items.

120. Artes textiles: Bijdragen tot de Geschiedenis van de Tapijt-, Borduur- en Textielkunst. (Centrum voor de Geschiedenis van de Tapijtkunst. Vereniging voor de Geschiedenis van de Textiele Kunsten.) Gent. 1953– . Irregular.

Each volume contains a critical bibliographic essay surveying articles and books published during a given period, primarily in Europe and North America, concerning the history of textile production as an art form in the Netherlands. The signed essay is organized by subject, e.g. *Tapijtkunst, Wandtapijten in Tentoonstellingen, Tapijten in Musea en Verzamelingen, Andere Wandbekledingen, Vloertapijten, Textiele Kunsten, Borduurkunst, Kant,* and *Kostuumgeschiedenis.* The subjects vary slightly with each volume. The essay is followed by a number of short signed reviews.

Examined: vol. 6 (1965), bibliography for 1960–62, *ca.* 300 items.

121. Ausgrabungen und Funde: Nachrichtenblatt für Vor- und Frühgeschichte. (Sektion für Vor- und Frühgeschichte, Deutsche Akademie der Wissenschaften zu Berlin.) Berlin. 1956– . Bimonthly.

The last number of each annual volume normally contains a bibliography of articles and books published during the previous year, principally in eastern Europe, concerning archaeology and the physical remnants of the past in Germanic and Slavic lands through the early Middle Ages. Classified by subject, chronological period, and geographic region. Occasional brief descriptive annotations.

Examined: vol. 10 (1965), bibliography for 1964–65, 642 items.

122. Bayerische Vorgeschichtsblätter. (Kommission für bayerische Landesgeschichte, Bayerische Akademie der Wissenschaften. Bayerische Landesamt für Denkmalpflege.) München. 1921– . Annual.

Continues **Bibliographie der bayerischen Vor- und Frühgeschichte 1884–1959.** F. Wagner, ed. (Kommission für bayerische Landesgeschichte, Bayerische Akademie der Wissenschaften.) Wiesbaden. 1964.

Each annual volume contains the "Schrifttum zur bayerischen Vor- und Frühgeschichte," a bibliography of articles and books recently published, primarily in Germany, concerning Bavarian archaeology from its prehistoric beginnings through the Carolingian period. The bibliography is meant to serve as an annual supplement to Wagner and is similarly organized by broad archaeological period. Bibliography began in 1963 for 1961–62.

Examined: vol. 30 (1965), bibliography for 1964–65, 191 items.

123. Bibliography of the Netherlands Institute for Art History. (Rijksbureau voor kunsthistorische Documentatie.) 's-Gravenhage. 1943– (publ. 1946–). Biennial.

Continues **Repertorium voor de Geschiedenis der Nederlandsche Schilder- en Graveerkunst.** H. van Hall, ed. 2 vols. 's-Gravenhage. 1936, 1949.

A bibliography of articles and books published during a given two-year period in Europe and North America, concerning Dutch and Flemish art (excluding architecture) from the Middle Ages to the present. Published in two parts: "Old Art" and "19th and 20th Centuries." The former is classified by topic within three major sections: *Painting, Sculpture,* and *Arts and Crafts.* Occasional brief descriptive annotations. Reviews are noted. Part II has been delayed for vols. 10–11.

Examined: vol. 11 (1961–62, publ. 1966), bibliography for 1961–62, 1,893 items (Part I only).

124. Bulletin signalétique: Domaines complémentaires; Préhistoire, archéologie et histoire de l'art ancien (à l'exception du domaine gréco-romain). (Centre national de la recherche scientifique.) Paris. 1966– . Quarterly.

Continues in part archaeological sections published 1947–66 in **Bulletin signalétique 23: Esthétique, archéologie, arts (230).**

A bibliography of articles recently published throughout the world concerning the art and archaeology of prehistory, the Middle Ages, the Orient, and pre-Columbian America. The publications are classified by topic under the following headings: *Généralités, Préhistoire, Civilisations anciennes du Moyen-Orient, Civilisations médiévales* (subdivided into Islam and Europe), *Asie orientale, Civilisations américaines.* Descriptive annotations (up to 150 words). This bibliography appears only as a section of the **Bulletin signalétique (5).** Annual author and subject indexes. This bibliography began in the last quarter of 1966.

Examined: vol. 20 (1966), bibliography for 1964–65, 765 items, *ca.* 2,500 serials indexed (for sections 19–24 of the **Bulletin**).

125. Commentari: Rivista di critica e storia dell'arte. Roma. 1950– . Semiannual.

Each number contains a bibliography of articles and books recently published in Europe and North America, concerning the history of Italian art from the Middle Ages to the present. The publications are classified by historical period.
Examined: vol. 17 (1966), bibliography for 1965–66, *ca.* 550 items.

126. COWA Bibliography: Current Publications in Old World Archaeology. (Council for Old World Archaeology.) Boston. 1957– . Irregular.

A bibliographic series which reports articles and books published during a given period in Europe and North America concerning the archaeology of Europe, Africa, Asia, and Australia. The series is composed of twenty-two sections, each of which is devoted to a given geographic area and is separately edited and published. Areas 1–10 concern Europe: British Isles, Scandinavia, Western Europe, Western Mediterranean, Central Europe, Balkans, Eastern Mediterranean, European Russia, Northeast Africa, Northwest Africa. The publications in each area are arranged by subject and archaeological period. Several of those noted above contain sections devoted to medieval archaeology. Descriptive annotations (up to 200 words). The Council also publishes the **COWA Survey,** a report of recent excavations in the field, similarly arranged in twenty-two sections, each of which is separately edited and published.
Examined: ser. 2 (1961–65), bibliography for 1957–61, 5,861 items.

127. Fasti archaeologici: Annual Bulletin of Classical Archaeology. (International Association for Classical Archaeology.) Firenze. 1946– (publ. 1948–). Annual.

Each volume comprises an extensive bibliography of articles and books published during a given year, principally in Europe, North America, and the Near East, concerning the study of Greco-Roman civilization through the physical remains of the past. The publications are arranged, along with archaeological news items, within an extensive subject and geographic classification under six major headings: *General, Prehistoric and Classical Greece, Italy before the Roman Empire, The Hellenistic*

*World and the Eastern Provinces of the Roman Empire, The
Roman West, Christianity and Late Antiquity.* Frequent descriptive or critical annotations (up to 400 words). Reviews
are noted. Indexes of ancient and modern authors, geographic
names, subjects, lexicalia, and literary and epigraphical sources.
Examined: vol. 17 (1962, publ. 1965), bibliography for 1962,
8,083 items.

128. Germania: Anzeiger der Römisch-germanischen Kommission des Deutschen archäologischen Instituts. (Römisch-
germanische Kommission des Deutschen archäologischen
Instituts, Frankfurt am Main.) Berlin. 1917– . Semiannual.

Each issue contains a list of current acquisitions of the Römisch-
germanische Kommission, namely articles and books recently
published in Europe and North America concerning ancient and
medieval European archaeology. Monographs and periodicals
are listed separately by author and serial title respectively. Select
tables of contents are given for series and periodicals. Annual
author index. Bibliography began in 1926.
Examined: vol. 44 (1966), accessions for 1965–66, 691
books, 776 periodicals.

129. Helinium: Revue consacrée à l'archéologie des Pays-Bas,
de la Belgique et du Grand Duché de Luxembourg. Wet-
teren. 1961– . Three issues yearly.

One issue of each annual volume normally contains a bibliography of articles and books published during a given year, primarily in western Europe, concerning the archaeology of the
Netherlands, Belgium, and Luxembourg from its prehistoric beginnings through the high Middle Ages. Publications are classified by subject and broad archaeological period: *Bibliographies,
répertoires et chroniques; Musées, expositions, conservation des
monuments; Méthodologie et sciences auxiliaires; Livres et articles traitant de plus d'une période; Paléolithique et mésolithique;
Néolithique; Age du bronze et âge du fer; Époque romaine;
Époque des migrations, époque mérovingienne et haut moyen
âge; Varia et personalia.* The bibliography in vol. 1 covered 1957–
58.
Examined: vol. 6 (1966), bibliography for 1965, 589 items.

130. Kölner Domblatt: Jahrbuch des Zentral-Dombauvereins. (Zentral-Dombauverein.) Köln. 1948– . Annual.

Each issue contains the "Dombibliographie," which lists articles and books recently published, primarily in Germany, concerning the history of the cathedral and archdiocese of Cologne from their foundations to the present. The publications are classified by subject under two headings: *Der Dom* (primarily devoted to the history of its art and architecture); and *Erzbischöfe und Domkapital.* Frequent descriptive annotations (up to 250 words). Examined: nos. 21–22 (1963), bibliography for 1962–63, 316 items.

131. Kunstgeschichtliche Anzeigen. (Kunsthistorisches Institut der Universität Wien. Institut für österreichische Geschichtsforschung.) Graz, Wien, and Köln. 1955– . Annual.

Continues **Kritische Berichte zur kunstgeschichtlichen Literatur.** Leipzig. 1927–38. And **Kunstgeschichtliche Anzeigen.** Wien. 1904–13.

Each issue comprises two or more signed critical review essays discussing articles and books published during a given period, principally in Europe and North America, concerning the art of a particular civilization, country, or period. Each essay is preceded by a list of the books discussed. Reviews are noted. Author index. Examined: vol. 6 (1963–64), five review essays for 1956–64.

132. Medieval Archaeology. (Society for Medieval Archaeology.) London. 1957– (publ. 1958–). Annual.

Each annual volume contains "Medieval Britain," a detailed report of archaeological excavations undertaken throughout Great Britain during a given year. The descriptions of excavations and finds are arranged by place under two major headings: *Pre-Conquest*, and *Post-Conquest* (subdivided into *Monastic Sites, Cathedrals and Ecclesiastical Palaces, Churches and Chapels, Castles, Towns, Royal Palaces, Manors and Moats, Farms and Smaller Domestic Architecture, Villages, Other Sites, Industry*). The individual descriptions (up to 600 words) are based on reports contributed by the excavators and are occasionally illustrated. References to publications resulting from these excavations are noted. Quinquennial general (objects, types of sites, persons, authors, authorities cited) and topographic indexes. Examined: vol. 9 (1965, publ. 1966), bibliography for 1964, *ca.* 200 reports.

*133. Répertoire d'art et d'archéologie. (Comité international d'histoire de l'art.) Paris. 1910– . Annual.

An extensive bibliography of articles and books published during the previous year, primarily in Europe and North America, concerning European art and archaeology since antiquity, and art (primarily Western) throughout the world in the twentieth century. The bibliography is divided into seven major sections: *Généralités; Art paléochrétien, byzantin et du Haut Moyen Age (Généralités, Art des migrations, Art chrétien d'Orient, Art chrétien d'Occident); Art roman et gothique (Généralités, Architecture et fouilles, Sculpture, Peinture et gravure, Arts décoratifs); Renaissance; XVIIe et XVIIIe siècles; XIXe siècle; XXe siècle.* Each of these is extensively subdivided by topic and geographic area. On completion of the volume for 1963 (publ. 1967), this bibliography ceased to cover ancient, Islamic, Indian, and Oriental art and archaeology (except for the present century). Frequent brief descriptive annotations (up to 50 words). Significant reviews are listed by reviewer. Indexes of artists and authors. Examined: ser. 2, vol. 2 (1966, publ. 1967), bibliography for 1966, 9,157 items, *ca.* 900 serials indexed.

*134. Rivista di archeologia cristiana. (Pontificia commissione di archeologia sacra. Pontificio istituto di archeologia cristiana.) Roma. 1924– . Semiannual.

One number of each annual volume contains the "Bibliografia dell' antichità cristiana," which includes articles and books recently published in Europe, the Near East, and North America concerning the history and archaeology of Christianity from its origins to the ninth century. Classified by topic, e.g. *Sussidi storici, Liturgia e culto dei santi, Agiografia, Sinagoghe, Iconografia, Vita monastica.* Occasional descriptive or critical annotations (up to 50 words). Author index. Bibliography began in 1929.

Examined: vol. 39 (1963), bibliography for 1961–62, 1,179 items, *ca.* 450 serials indexed.

135. Schrifttum zur deutschen Kunst. (Deutscher Verein für Kunstwissenschaft. Bibliothek des germanischen Nationalmuseums.) Berlin. 1933– (publ. 1934–). Annual.

Each volume comprises an extensive bibliography of articles and books published during a given year, primarily in Germany, concerning all aspects of German art, from its origins to the present. Classified into three major sections: I. *Grundriss der Forschung (Schrifttumsverzeichnisse, Gelehrte Gesellschaften . . . , Gelehrtengeschichte . . . , Wissenschaftsgeschichte . . .)*; II. *Bausteine des Wissens (Nachschlagewerke, Quellenwerke, Landeskunde . . . , Denkmalpflege und Museum, Ikonographie)*; III. *Aufbau der Kunstgeschichte (Die deutsche Kunst und ihre Landschaften, Die Zeiten, Die Künste: Baukunst, Skulptur, Wand- und Tafelmalerei, Glasmalerei, Buchmalerei, Zeichnung, Druckgraphik und Buchillustration, Ornamentik, Kunsthandwerk)*. Brief descriptive annotations. Book reviews are noted. Indexes of artists, places, and authors.

Examined: vol. 27 (1963, publ. 1965), bibliography for 1963, 1,825 items.

136. Zeitschrift für Kunstgeschichte. München and Berlin. 1932– . Three issues yearly.

The last number of each annual volume contains an extensive bibliography of articles and books published during the previous year in Europe and North America concerning the history of art, principally in Europe, from its origins to the present. Publications are classified by topic and medium, subdivided by country, e.g. *Ikonographie; Baukunst; Ornamentik . . . ; Malerei und Graphik; Mosaiken; Buchmalerei; Glasmalerei; Metall, Email, Edelstein; Elfenbein; Textilien.* Reviews are noted. Author index. Each issue also contains one or more "Literaturberichte" or review articles surveying publication on an important subject of art history.

Examined: vol. 28 (1965), bibliography for 1964, 2,779 items.

See also:

VI. Ecclesiastical History

A. General

137. Archives de sociologie des religions. (Groupe de sociologie des religions, Centre national de la recherche scientifique.) Paris. 1956– . Semiannual.

Each issue contains a bibliography of articles and books recently published in Europe and North America concerning the sociological study of religions, especially Christianity. The publications are listed alphabetically by author in two parts: articles and monographic publications. Descriptive or critical annotations (up to 1,000 words).

Examined: vol. 11 (1966), bibliography for 1965–66, 549 items.

138. Catholic Historical Review. (Catholic University of America.) Washington, D.C. 1915– . Quarterly.

Each number contains a bibliography of articles recently published, principally in Europe and North America, concerning the history of the Christian churches from their beginnings to the present. Publications are classified by historical period. The bibliography began in 1923.

Examined: vol. 50 (1964–65), bibliography for 1963–64, *ca.* 750 items.

139. International Bibliography of the History of Religions. Bibliographie internationale de l'histoire des religions. (International Association for the History of Religions.) Leiden. 1952– (publ. 1954–). Annual.

Each volume comprises a bibliography of articles and books published during a given year throughout the world concerning the history of all religions. The material is arranged by topic within eight major sections: *General Works, Prehistoric and Primitive Religions, Religions of Antiquity, Judaism and Ancient Israel, Christianity, Islam, Hinduism, East Asian Religions.* Reviews are noted. Index of ancient and modern authors.

Examined: 1962 (publ. 1964), bibliography for 1962, *ca.* 1,200 items.

140. Répertoire général de sciences religieuses. (Centre d'études Saint-Louis-de-France, Roma.) Paris. 1950– (publ. 1953–). Annual.

Each issue comprises an extensive bibliography of articles and books published during a given year throughout the world concerning the study and practice of all religions, with emphasis on the Judeo-Christian tradition. The publications are arranged according to an extensive subject classification, covering most aspects of ecclesiastical and religious studies. Among these are the history of religions (including Islam and Judaism), biblical studies, Catholic theology (including mariology, pilgrimages, and liturgy), Christian authors (including patristics), philosophy, canon law, ecclesiastical history, art and archaeology (including Byzantine, Coptic, and Islamic), religious and military orders, hagiography, biography, religious literature, and music. Indexes of authors and anonymous works.

Examined: 1957 (publ. 1965), bibliography for 1957, 20,528 items, *ca.* 1,250 serials indexed.

*141. Revue d'histoire ecclésiastique: Bibliographie. (Université catholique de Louvain.) Louvain. 1900– . Three issues yearly.

An extensive annual bibliography of articles and books recently published throughout the world concerning the history of the Church. The four major divisions of the bibliography are: *Sciences auxiliaires,* subdivided by topic; *Publications de sources et critique des sources,* subdivided by topic; *Travaux historiques,* subdivided by chronological period (patristic, medieval, modern, and contemporary) and by topic (institutions, law, Church, liturgy, hagiography, science and letters, art, economy and society); *Comptes rendus d'ouvrages précédemment annoncés*, comprising a list of recent reviews of items previously noted. Occasional brief descriptive annotations. Reviews are included. Each issue of the **Revue** itself also contains a "Chronique," which is an extensive report on current periodical and monographic publication of any format arranged by country of origin. The larger sections are subdivided by topic, e.g. *Bibliographies, Catalogues, Publications de sources et travaux*. Each item is accompanied by a signed descriptive or critical annotation of up to 500 words. Annual index of authors and names to the "Chronique" and the **Bibliographie.**

Examined: vol. 61 (1966), bibliography for 1963–66, 10,221 items, *ca.* 750 serials indexed.

142. Zeitschrift für die neutestamentliche Wissenschaft und die Kunde der älteren Kirche. Berlin. 1900– . Semiannual.

Each issue contains a bibliography of articles recently published in Europe and North America concerning the early church and New Testament studies. The publications are classified by topic under the following headings: *Ausserbiblische Religionsgeschichte . . . , Die Bibel als Ganzes, Das alte Testament . . . , Das neue Testament . . . , Neutestamentliche Einleitung . . . , Das Urchristentum, Die alte Kirche.* The patristic section is subdivided by historical period and subject. Bibliography began in 1957.

Examined: vol. 58 (1967), bibliography for 1966–67, *ca.* 700 items, 42 serials indexed.

See also:

    10. International Bibliography of Historical Sciences
    127. Fasti archaeologici
    134. Rivista di archeologia cristiana
    210. Bibliographia patristica
    214. Bulletin signalétique 19: Philosophie, sciences religieuses
    217. Estudios eclesiásticos

B. Eastern Church

143. Aegyptus: Rivista italiana di egittologia e di papirologia. (Scuola di papirologia, Università cattolica del Sacro Cuore.) Milano. 1920– . Semiannual.

Each issue contains the "Bibliografia metodica degli studi di egittologia e di papirologia," which includes articles and books recently published in Europe and North America concerning all aspects of Egyptology and papyrology. While the emphasis is heavily pre-Christian, there usually are a number of items on Coptic studies and early patristic thought and letters. Publications are classified by general topic. Reviews are noted.

Examined: vol. 45 (1965), bibliography for 1964–65, 975 items.

144. Bibliographie copte. (Pontificium institutum biblicum.) Roma. 1952– (publ. 1953–) Annual.

Published as a separately paginated supplement in **Orientalia: Commentarii trimestres.** (Pontificium institutum biblicum.) Roma.

Continues annual "Bibliographie copte" in **Orientalia,** 1949–52.

Each volume comprises a bibliography of articles and books published during the previous year in Europe, North America, and the Near East concerning Coptic history. Classified by topic, e.g. *Bible, Apocryphes; Gnosticisme, Manichéisme; Littérature; Monachisme; Hagiographie; Liturgie, théologie; Linguistique, philologie.* Occasional brief descriptive annotations. Reviews are noted. Current reviews of books listed in the previous bibliographies are noted in a separate section. Author index.

Examined: vol. 16 (1963, publ. 1964), bibliography for 1963, 182 items; in **Orientalia,** ser. 2, vol. 33 (1964).

145. Ostkirchliche Studien. (Arbeitsgemeinschaft der deutschen Augustinerordensprovinz zum Studium der Ostkirche.) Würzburg. 1952– . Quarterly.

Each number contains one installment of a bibliography of articles and books published recently in Europe (particularly Central and eastern Europe) and North America concerning the cultural, political, and especially the ecclesiastical history of Russia, the Slavic countries, Greece, Turkey, Egypt, and the Middle East from antiquity to the present. The bibliography begins anew upon the completion of one subject sequence. The publications are normally classified in five major sections: *Theologie* (subdivided into *Dogmatik, Mariendogma, Moral und Pastoral, Exegese, Patrologie, Liturgik, Kirchenrecht, Mönchtum, Frömmigkeitsgeschichte, Hagiographie, Oikumene), Philosophie und Literatur, Geschichte, Kunstgeschichte und Archäologie, Kommunismus*. Occasional descriptive annotations (up to 50 words). Annual author index.

Examined: vol. 16 (1967), bibliography for 1962–66, *ca.* 1,400 items.

146. Studia orientalia christiana: Collectanea; Studi, documenti, bibliografia. (Centro francescano di studi orientali cristiani.) Cairo. 1956– . Annual.

Continues bibliography in **Aegyptiaca christiana, Sezione III:** Collectanea. (Seminario francescano orientale, Al-Gīzah.) Cairo. 1957–58.

Each annual volume contains the "Bibliografia copta," the "Bibliografia greca," and the "Bibliografia armena." These three include articles and books published during the preceding year, primarily in the Near East, concerning the history and theology of the Coptic, Greek Orthodox, and Armenian churches. Each is classified by topic including: *Dommatica, Sacra scrittura, Morale, Diritto, Liturgia, Pastorale, Ascetica, Storia* (subdivided by topic), *Varia*. Reviews are noted. Titles in Arabic, Greek, and Armenian are also given in Italian. The Coptic bibliography began in 1958, the Greek bibliography in 1964, and the Armenian in 1965.

Examined: vol. 10 (1965), bibliography for 1964, Coptic 536 items, Greek 111 items, Armenian 171 items.

See also:
23. **Orientalistische Literaturzeitung**
210. **Bibliographia patristica**
225. **Theología**
   Section III-A, Byzantium

C. Monasticism and the Religious Orders

147. Analecta praemonstratensia. (Commissio historica Ordinis praemonstratensis, Abbatia Averbodiensis.) Tongerloo. 1925– . Semiannual.

Each number contains a section "Chronicon," which comprises a bibliography of articles and books recently published, principally in Europe, concerning the Premonstratensians from their origins to the present. The publications are normally arranged under four headings: *Generalia, Hagiographica, Auctores antiqui, Particularia* (individual Premonstratensian houses). Initialed descriptive annotations (up to 500 words).
Examined: vol. 40 (1964), bibliography for 1962–64, *ca.* 175 items.

148. Archivum bibliographicum carmelitanum. Roma. 1955– (publ. 1956–). Annual.
Published as a supplement to **Ephemerides carmeliticae.** Roma.

Each annual volume contains the "Bibliographia carmeli teresiani," which includes articles and books published during a given year throughout the world, written principally by Carmelites or Discalced Carmelites, concerning various aspects of Christian spirituality and Carmelite history up to the present. The publications are classified by topic under seven headings: *Opera generalia, Philosophia, Religio . . . , Scientiae sociales . . . , Artes pulchrae, Litterae, Historia et biographia profana. . . .* Frequent brief descriptive annotations. Reviews are noted; those for items previously listed are noted in the appendix. Index of names.
Examined: vol. 8 (1962, publ. 1965), bibliography for 1962, 1,252 items.

149. Augustiniana: Tijdschrift voor de Studie van Sint Augustinus en de Augustijnenorde. Revue pour l'étude de Saint Augustin et de l'Ordre des Augustins. (Institutum historicum augustinianum Lovanii.) Louvain. 1951 . Semiannual.

This journal occasionally contains the "Bibliographie d'histoire augustinienne," which includes articles and books recently published in Europe and North America concerning the Augustinian Order from its origins to the present. The publications are classified under the following headings: *Histoire de l'Ordre* (subdivided by country), *Missions, Hagiographie, Spiritualité et dévotions, Auteurs* (subdivided by century). Frequent brief descriptive annotations. Reviews are noted. Bibliography began in 1952. This journal also publishes the "Répertoire bibliographique de Saint Augustin" **(207)**.

Examined: vol. 15 (1965), bibliography for 1960–64, 532 items.

*150. Bibliographia franciscana. (Istituto storico dei Fratres Minori Cappuccini.) Roma. 1938–   (publ. 1943–   ). Irregular.

Published as a supplement to **Collectanea franciscana.** (Istituto storico dei Fratres Minori Cappuccini.) Roma.

Continues "Bibliographia franciscana" in **Collectanea franciscana,** 1931–42.

Each volume comprises an extensive bibliography of articles and books published throughout the world during a given period concerning all aspects of the Franciscan Order and its members, from 1226 to the present. Publications are classified under seven major headings: *Subsidia et instrumenta; Relationes de S. Francisco; Relationes de studiis, doctrinis et scriptoribus franciscanis; Relationes de historia primi ordinis franciscani; Relationes de secundo ordine S. Francisci seu de ordine S. Clarae; Relationes de tertio ordine S. Francisci; Relationes de arte franciscana.* Each of these is subdivided by topic or geographic region. Frequent initialed descriptive or critical annotations (up to 500 words.) Reviews are noted. Index of persons and places.

Examined: vol. 11 (1954–57, publ. 1959–65), bibliography for 1954–57, 4,623 items.

*151. Bulletin d'histoire bénédictine. (Abbaye de Maredsous.) Maredsous. 1907–   . Irregular.

Published as a separately paginated supplement to **Revue bénédictine.** (Abbaye de Maredsous.) Maredsous.

Each volume comprises an extensive bibliography of articles and books recently published, primarily in Europe and North America, concerning Benedictine monasticism, from its origins to the present. In vols. 1–5, the publications were classified by topic or geographic area under three major headings: *Monachisme primitif, Monachisme celtique,* and *Monachisme bénédictin.* Beginning with vol. 6, publications are classified under two headings: *Monachisme pré-bénédictin,* which contains only those studies of particular relevance to the Benedictine movement, and *Monachisme bénédictin,* which forms the major portion of the bibliography and is subdivided by geographic area. The series of topics is repeated upon completion of one subject sequence, three or four of which normally constitute one volume of the **Bulletin.** Frequent descriptive or critical annotations (up to 500 words). Author and extensive subject indexes at the end of each volume.

Examined: vol. 6 (1957–63), bibliography for 1954–62, 2,474 items.

*152. **Bulletin d'histoire monastique.** (Abbaye Saint-Martin.) Ligugé. 1936– . Irregular.

Published as a separately paginated supplement in **Revue Mabillon:** Archives de la France monastique. (Abbaye Saint-Martin.) Ligugé.

Continues "Chronique bibliographique" (often separately paginated) in **Revue Mabillon,** 1905–35.

Each volume comprises an extensive bibliography of articles and books recently published, principally in Europe and North America, concerning the history of monastic institutions, particularly in France. The publications are classified under the following major headings: *Généralités et institutions, Les origines monastiques, Le monachisme en France, Topobibliographie monastique* (by order of the ecclesiastical provinces of France — Paris, Reims, Cambrai, Rouen, etc.). The series of topics is repeated upon completion of one subject sequence. Frequent descriptive or critical annotations (up to 150 words).

Examined: vol. 5 (1944–58), bibliography for 1938–58, 3,596 items.

153. **Carmelus:** Commentarii ab instituto carmelitano editi. (Institutum carmelitanum.) Roma. 1954– . Semiannual.

The second issue of each annual volume contains the "Bibliographia carmelitana annualis," which includes articles and books

published during the preceding year throughout the world, and written either by Carmelites or about the Carmelite Order. Classified by topic. Frequent descriptive annotations (up to 250 words). Index of names.
Examined: vol. 12 (1965), bibliography for 1964, 937 items.

154. Cîteaux: Commentarii cistercienses. (Abbatia Westmallensis.) Westmalle. 1950– . Quarterly.
Entitled **Cîteaux in de Nederlanden,** 1950–58.

Two numbers of each annual volume normally contain a bibliography of articles and books published during the last several years, principally in Europe, concerning primarily the Cistercian monastic movement up to the present. The publications are classified by topic, e.g. *Spiritualia, Monastica, Historica,* one of which is normally included in each issue. Initialed descriptive or critical annotations (up to 1,500 words).
Examined: vol. 17 (1966), bibliography for 1962–65, *ca.* 175 items.

155. Collectanea cisterciensia. Westmalle. 1934– . Quarterly.
Entitled **Collectanea ordinis cisterciensium reformatorum,** 1934–1964.

Each number contains one section of the annual "Bulletin de spiritualité monastique," which is a critical bibliographic essay discussing articles and books recently published in Europe and North America concerning monastic life and institutions and, in particular, monastic spiritualism. The publications are grouped and discussed by topic within broad chronological divisions. Annual index of names. Bibliography began in 1960. Since 1967, the "Bulletin" has been published in English in **Cistercian Studies.**
Examined: vol. 29 (1967), bibliography for 1965–66, 242 items.

D. Western Church

156. Archief voor de Geschiedenis van de Katholieke Kerk in Nederland. Utrecht and Antwerpen. 1959– . Three issues yearly.

The third number of each annual volume contains a bibliography of articles and books recently published, principally in the

Netherlands, concerning the history of Catholicism in the Netherlands through the present. The publications are classified by topic and geographic region, including *devotio moderna*, humanism, and monastic history. Occasional brief descriptive annotations. Reviews are noted. Author index. The bibliography began in 1960.

Examined: vol. 6 (1964), bibliography for 1962–63, 113 items.

157. Archivum historiae pontificiae. (Facultas historiae ecclesiasticae, Pontificia Universitas Gregoriana.) Roma. 1963– . Annual.

Each volume contains an extensive bibliography of articles and books published throughout the world during a given period concerning the history of the papacy and, for the early centuries, the history of Christianity in Rome. The material is listed under the relevant pope from St. Peter through Paul VI, with subdivision by topic when warranted. General works are listed together at the beginning of either the whole bibliography or of a specific historical epoch. Reviews are noted; those for items previously listed are noted at the end of each section. Author and subject indexes.

Examined: vol. 3 (1965), bibliography for 1964–65, 3,171 items, *ca.* 600 serials indexed.

158. Revue d'histoire de l'église de France. (Société d'histoire ecclésiastique de la France.) Paris. 1910– . Annual.

Each volume contains several bibliographic sections which together report recent periodical and monographic publications in France, Europe, and North America concerning the Church in France from its origins to the present. The principal section is "Recueils et périodiques généraux" or "Recueils et périodiques régionaux," a list of articles drawn from the major general or regional journals in the field. The articles are listed by journal title. The general and regional journals are surveyed in alternate years, and are arranged by country and institution of origin or by local region respectively. Occasional brief descriptive annotations. This section complements the "Bulletin critique" and "Notes bibliographiques," which contain reviews of current monographic publications. The latter section is organized by historical period and topic.

Examined: vol. 52 (1966), bibliography for 1965–66, 42 journals.

159. Rivista di storia della chiesa in Italia. Roma. 1947– .
Three issues yearly.

Each number normally contains a bibliography of articles and books recently published in Europe and North America concerning the history of the Church, especially in Italy, from its origins to the present. The publications are classified in two major sections: *Storia generale,* which is subdivided by chronological period, and *Storia locale,* which is subdivided by geographic region within Italy. Descriptive annotations (up to 100 words). Author index.

Examined: vol. 18 (1964), bibliography for 1961–63, 820 items.

See also:
   70. Bibliografia romana
   105. Bibliografia dell'Archivio Vaticano
   108. Quellen und Forschungen aus italienischen Archiven und Bibliotheken
   210. Bibliographia patristica

VII. Economic, Social, and Institutional History

A. Economics and Agriculture

160. The Agricultural History Review. (British Agricultural History Society.) London. 1953– . Semiannual.

The first issue of each annual volume normally contains a bibliography of articles and books published during the previous year, principally in Great Britain, concerning agrarian history in Great Britain from pre-Roman times to the present. Publications are listed by author in two series, *Books and Pamphlets* and *Articles*. Occasionally the second number contains lists of work in progress in the United Kingdom and, to a limited degree, in the Commonwealth.

Examined: vol. 15 (1967), bibliography for 1965–66, *ca.* 250 items.

161. Bibliographia historiae rerum rusticarum internationalis. (Magyar Mezögazdasági Múzeum.) Budapest. 1964– . Annual.

Continues annual bibliography published 1957–63 in **Agrártörténeti szemle. Historia rerum rusticarum.** (Agrártörténeti Bizottság, Magyar Tudományos Akadémia.) Budapest.

79

Each annual volume comprises an extensive bibliography of articles and books recently published primarily in Europe and North America concerning agrarian history throughout the world from antiquity to the present. The bibliography is organized by subject: *Bibliographies relating to the history of agriculture; Methods of agricultural history; The history of agricultural historiography; General works* (subdivided into economic and social history); *Agricultural production and the technology and technique of production* (subdivided by type of agricultural production); *Agrareconomies; Agrarian society; Agricultural policy; Agrarian law; Agricultural administration; Agricultural education.* English translations are given for titles not in the major western European languages. Indexes of countries and of authors.

Examined: 1962–63 (publ. 1965), bibliography for 1962–63, 4,736 items.

162. The Economic History Review. (Economic History Society.) London. 1927– . Three issues yearly.

One number of each annual volume normally contains a list of articles and books published during a given year, principally in the United Kingdom, concerning the economic history of Great Britain and Ireland. Publications are listed alphabetically by author within three sections: *Original Documents, Books and Pamphlets*, and *Articles in Periodicals.*

Examined: ser. 2, vol. 19 (1966), bibliography for 1964, *ca.* 700 items.

*163. Hansische Geschichtsblätter. (Hansische Geschichtsverein.) Köln. 1871– . Annual.

Each volume contains the "Hansische Umschau," which comprises a bibliography of articles and books recently published throughout the world concerning the role of the Hansa in European commercial and economic history from the early Middle Ages to the present. Publications are classified by topic and geographic region within seven major sections: *Allgemeines und hansische Gesamtgeschichte, Vorhansische Zeit, Zur Geschichte der einzelnen Hansestädte und der niederdeutschen Landschaften, Westeuropa, Skandinavien, Osteuropa, Hanseatische Wirtschafts- und Überseegeschichte.* Each item is accom-

panied by an initialed discussion of up to 1,000 words. Author index. The bibliography began in 1921.
Examined: vol. 85 (1967), bibliography for 1966, *ca.* 500 items.

164. Historia agriculturae. (Nederlands agronomisch-historisch Instituut.) Groningen. 1953– . Annual.

Each annual volume contains a bibliography of articles and books published during a given period, principally in Europe and North America, concerning agricultural history throughout the world from antiquity to the present. Classified by country and geographic region. Occasional brief descriptive annotations.
Examined: vol. 85 (1967), bibliography for 1966, *ca.* 500 items.

165. International Bibliography of Economics. Bibliographie internationale de science économique. (International Committee for Social Sciences Documentation.) London and Chicago. 1952– (publ. 1955–). Annual.
Part of **International Bibliography of the Social Sciences. Bibliographie internationale des sciences sociales.**

An extensive bibliography of articles and books published during a given year throughout the world concerning economic history, theory, and current developments. Classified by topic, historical period, or geographic area within major subject divisions. While the focus of the bibliography is primarily modern, there is medieval material in the sections devoted to the history of economic thought and to economic history. Occasional brief descriptive annotations. Reviews are noted. English translations are given for titles not in French or English. Author and subject indexes.
Examined: vol. 14 (1965, publ. 1966), bibliography for 1965, 7,167 items, *ca.* 1,500 serials indexed.

166. Roczniki Dziejów społecznych i gospodarczych. Annales d'histoire sociale et économique. (Wydział Historii i Nauk Społecznych, Poznańskie Towarzystwo Przyjaciół Nauk.) Poznań. 1931– . Annual.

Each volume contains a bibliography of articles and books recently published, primarily in Europe and North America, concerning social and economic history from antiquity to the present. The publications are arranged by language within twelve major subject divisions. Extensive reviews of significant books normally appear at the beginning of each of these divisions. Examined: vol. 27 (1965, publ. 1966), bibliography for 1963–64, *ca.* 1,100 items, 35 books reviewed.

167. Srednie veka: Sbornik [Middle Ages: Collectanea]. (Institut istorii, Akademiia nauk SSSR.) Moskva. 1942– . Annual.

Each annual volume contains a bibliography of articles and books published in the U.S.S.R. during a given year concerning the Middle Ages in western Europe, Hungary, and Romania, with emphasis on economic and social history. The publications are classified by country or topic within four sections: I. *The Middle Ages as a Whole*; II. *The Formation of Feudalism, 400–1100*; III. *Developed Feudalism, 1100–1500*; IV. *The Breakup of Feudalism, 1500–1650.* Examined: vol. 30 (1967), bibliography for 1964, 227 items.

See also:
    7. Deutsches Archiv für Erforschung des Mittelalters
  10. International Bibliography of Historical Sciences
  54. Bremisches Jahrbuch
 141. Revue d'histoire ecclésiastique: Bibliographie
 274. Bulletin signalétique 22: Histoire des sciences et des techniques
 277. Isis
 283. Technology and Culture
    Section IV-C, Numismatics

B. Geography and Cartography

168. Bibliographie cartographique internationale. (Comité national français de géographie. Union géographique internationale.) Paris. 1936– (publ. 1938–). Annual.
    Entitled **Bibliographie cartographique française,** 1937–38; **Bibliographie cartographique de la France,** 1936.

An extensive bibliography of maps and atlases published recently throughout the world. The maps and atlases are classified by continent, country, and local region. Historical maps and atlases are listed under the geographic area which they depict. Occasional brief descriptive annotations. Indexes of authors, publishers and printers, and subjects. Examined: 1964 (publ. 1966), bibliography for 1964, 2,652 items.

*169. Bibliographie géographique internationale. (Association de géographes français. Union géographique internationale.) Paris. 1915– (publ. 1921–). Annual.
Continues "Bibliographie géographique annuelle," 1891–1914, published 1892–1915 in **Annales de géographie.** Paris.

An extensive bibliography of articles, books, and atlases recently published throughout the world concerning all aspects of geography. The bibliography is divided into two major sections. The first section is *Partie générale,* which is classified by subject: *Méthodes et enseignement de la géographie, Histoire des sciences géographiques, Histoire des découvertes géographiques, Géographie historique* (the last three contain sections devoted to ancient, medieval, and early modern geography, and the four are indexed by subject, historical person, and geographic name), *Cartographie, Morphologie et sciences annexes, Météorologie, Hydrologie, Biogéographie, Géographie humaine, Bibliographies.* . . . The second section is *Partie régionale,* which is classified by continent, country, and geographic topic or region. Reviews are noted. Frequent signed descriptive annotations (up to 250 words). Author index.
Examined: vol. 70 (1964, publ. 1966), bibliography for 1964, *ca.* 7,250 items.

170. Geographical Abstracts. (London School of Economics.) London. 1960– . Six issues yearly.

An extensive collection of abstracts of articles and books published recently in Europe and North America concerning all aspects of geography. Four separate sections, each published six times a year, make up an annual volume: A. *Geomorphology;* B. *Biogeography, Climatology & Cartography;* C. *Economic Geography;* D. *Social Geography.* Each is arranged by subject. The last two sections, in particular, contain material on historical geography. Annual author and regional indexes for each section. A keyword subject index to section A, 1960–65, was published in 1966. A similar keyword subject index for all four sections is planned on an annual basis. Sections B–D began in 1966.

Examined: 1966, bibliography for 1965, 4,854 abstracts.

171. Imago mundi: A Review of Early Cartography. Amsterdam. 1935–   . Annual.

Each annual volume contains a brief list of articles and books recently published, primarily in Europe and North America, concerning historical cartography. The publications are listed alphabetically by author.

Examined: vol. 19 (1965), bibliography for 1963–64, *ca.* 250 items.

C. Law and Institutions

*172. Annali della Fondazione italiana per la storia amministrativa. (Fondazione italiana per la storia amministrativa.) Milano. 1964–   . Annual.

Part four of each annual volume contains the "Bibliografia periodica sistematica internazionale di storia amministrativa," an extensive bibliography of articles and books recently published in Europe and the western hemisphere concerning Western administrative history, from the Roman period to the present century. The bibliography treats the history of institutions (especially public institutions), constitutional history, history of law (particularly public law), economic history (particularly public finance), social history (particularly social demography), history of political doctrine, history of economic doctrine. Publications are listed alphabetically by author. Five extensive indexes: *Cronologico* (a chronological index subdivided by geographic region), *Topografico* (a geographic index subdivided by chronological period), *Istituzionale* (an institutional index in two parts, *Sistematico* — by type of administrative institution, and *Alfabetico* — specific institution by title), *Persone e idee* (names of administrators, names of administrative theorists, and administrative

doctrines), *Metodologia e discipline strumentali* (index of methodology and auxiliary sciences).
Examined: vol. 1 (1964), bibliography for 1960–62, 2,988 items, *ca.* 250 serials indexed.

173. Annali di storia del diritto. (Istituto di storia del diritto italiano. Scuola di perfezionamento nella storia del diritto medievale e moderno, Università di Roma.) Milano. 1957– . Annual.

This journal periodically contains the "Bibliografia italiana di storia del diritto medievale e moderno," which includes articles and books published during a given period, principally in Italy, concerning the history of customal, Roman, and, to a limited extent, canon law from the Middle Ages to the present. The publications are classified in four major sections: *Bibliografia in generale, Fonti in generale, Bibliografia e fonti per località,* and *Letteratura.* Reviews are noted. Extensive author and subject index. Bibliography was published in 1958 (for 1951–53) and 1959–60 (for 1954–56).
Examined: vol. 7 (1963), bibliography for 1957–59, 2,895 items, *ca.* 350 serials indexed.

174. Annual Legal Bibliography. (Harvard Law School Library.) Cambridge, Massachusetts. 1960– (publ. 1961–). Annual.
Cumulated from **Current Legal Bibliography.** (Harvard Law School Library.) Cambridge, Massachusetts. Monthly.

An extensive bibliography of recent acquisitions of the Harvard Law School Library, consisting of articles and books recently published throughout the world concerning law and legal studies. The bibliography is divided into four parts: *Common Law Jurisdictions; Civil Law and Other Jurisdictions; Private International Law, International Transactions; Public International Law.* Each is extensively subdivided according to legal topic. The first two parts contain sections devoted to legal history subdivided into *Primary Sources, Customary and Primitive Law, Roman Law, Feudal Law, Slavery.* Subject indexes in Spanish, German, French, and English.
Examined: vol. 6 (1965–66, publ. 1966), accessions for 1965–66, *ca.* 33,500 items, *ca.* 1,000 serials indexed.

175. Apollinaris: Commentarius iuris canonici. (Institutum utriusque iuris, Pontificia Universitas Lateranensis.) Città del Vaticano. 1928– . Quarterly.

Each annual volume contains a bibliography of articles and books published during the previous year in Europe and North America concerning canon law and its implementation up to the present. The publications are classified by topic. Author index. Examined: vol. 37 (1964), bibliography for 1963, *ca.* 300 items.

176. Archiv für katholisches Kirchenrecht. (Kanonistisches Institut der Universität München.) Mainz. 1857– . Semiannual.

Each issue contains a bibliography of articles and books recently published throughout the world concerning the history, study, and application of canon law. The publications are classified by topic under seven subject headings: *Allgemeines, Kirchenrechtsgeschichte, Geltendes Recht, Ostkirche, Konzilsfragen, Staat und Kirche,* and *Evangelisches Kirchenrecht.* The bibliography began in 1913. Examined: vol. 134 (1965), bibliography for 1964–65, *ca.* 750 items.

177. Bibliographie en langue française d'histoire du droit. Paris. 1926– (publ. 1958–). Annual.
    Entitled **Éléments de bibliographie sur l'histoire des institutions et des faits sociaux, 987–1875,** 1958.

An extensive bibliography of articles and books published in the French language during a given year concerning the history of Roman, civil, and canon law in France from the fifth to the twentieth century. Publications are listed alphabetically by author. Extensive subject index. Bibliography in vol. 1 includes works published 1926–56; bibliography in vol. 2, 1957–59. Examined: vol. 6 (1963, publ. 1966), bibliography for 1963, 1,670 items, *ca.* 400 serials indexed.

178. Canon Law Abstracts: A Half-Yearly Review of Periodical Literature in Canon Law. (Canon Law Society of Great Britain.) Melrose, Scotland. 1959– . Semiannual.

Each issue comprises a bibliography of articles and case reports published during a given period throughout the world concerning canon law. Emphasis is on the modern corpus, but the section *General and Historical Subjects* surveys material pertinent to medieval canon law. Abstracts of up to 325 words.

Examined: nos. 15–16 (1966), bibliography for 1965, *ca.* 600 items, *ca.* 50 serials abstracted.

179. Index to Foreign Legal Periodicals. (American Association of Law Libraries. Institute of Advanced Legal Studies, University of London.) London. 1960– . Quarterly.

Each issue comprises an extensive bibliography of articles recently published throughout the world concerning legal studies of all countries except those whose legal systems have a common-law basis, such as Great Britain and the United States. The publications are extensively classified by subject in dictionary form. Reviews are listed in a separate section by the author being reviewed. Inclusion of festschriften and volumes of essays began in 1963. Indexes of countries and geographic regions and of authors (including reviewers). Three quarterly issues are replaced by a cumulative annual volume which includes new publications of the fourth quarter. A triennial cumulation replaces the three annual volumes.

Examined: vol. 7 (1966), bibliography for 1965–66, *ca.* 7,500 articles, *ca.* 1,000 book reviews, *ca.* 350 serials indexed.

180. Index to Legal Periodicals. (American Association of Law Libraries.) New York. 1908– (publ. 1909–). Eleven issues yearly.

Each issue comprises an extensive bibliography of articles recently published in the United States, Canada, England, Scotland, Northern Ireland, Australia, and New Zealand concerning legal studies. The articles are extensively classified by subject in dictionary form. The emphasis is on modern law and its administration and practice. Reviews are listed in a separate section by the author being reviewed. Cumulations are published annually and triennially.

Examined: 1964–65 (publ. 1965), bibliography for 1964–65, *ca.* 30,000 articles, *ca.* 1,000 reviews, *ca.* 300 serials indexed.

181. International Bibliography of Political Science. Bibliographie internationale de science politique. (International Committee for Social Sciences Documentation.) London and Chicago. 1952– (publ. 1954–). Annual.
Part of **International Bibliography of the Social Sciences. Bibliographie internationale des sciences sociales.**

An extensive bibliography of articles and books published during a given year, throughout the world, concerning political theory and government. Classified extensively by subject, historical period, or geographic area within six major subject divisions: *Political Science, Political Thought, Government and Public Administration, Governmental Process, International Relations, Area Studies.* The emphasis of the bibliography is modern. Occasional brief descriptive annotations. Reviews are noted. Author and subject indexes.
    Examined: vol. 13 (1964, publ. 1965), bibliography for 1964, 4,293 items, *ca.* 1,500 serials indexed.

182. Iura: Rivista internazionale di diritto romano e antico. Napoli. 1950– . Semiannual.

The second part of each annual volume contains an extensive bibliography of articles and books recently published throughout the world concerning ancient law, primarily Roman, and its influences and effects. Classified by topic into twenty-one major sections (including an extensive section on ancient and medieval history). Book reviews are listed by reviewer. A list of the principal periodicals dealing with ancient law and the contents of their recent issues are also included. Frequent descriptive or critical annotations (up to 750 words). Index of authors and legal sources.
    Examined: vol. 16 (1965), bibliography for 1964, 2,515 items.

183. Répertoire bibliographique du droit belge. (Faculté de droit, Université de Liège). Liège. 1919– (publ. 1947–). Irregular.

An extensive bibliography of articles published in Belgium during a given period concerning legal history, practice, and theory. The publications are classified by subject within twenty-four sections. The historical section, *Droit ancien*, is divided into *Droit romain, Droit médiéval et modern, Droit civil, Droit commercial et économique, Organization judiciaire, Droit pénal, Procedure pénale, Droit publique et administratif, Droit fiscal et finances publiques, Droit canonique.* Note also the historical topics under *Droit étranger* and *Droit comparé.* The balance of the bibliography is devoted to contemporary law. Author and subject indexes. Bibliography for 1919–45 (publ. 1947); bibliography for 1946–55 (publ. 1957).

Examined: 1956–60 (publ. 1962), bibliography for 1956–60, 4,509 items, 112 serials indexed.

184. Revue historique de droit français et étranger. Paris. 1855– . Quarterly.

In each issue the section "Chronique" contains part of a bibliographic survey of recent publications concerning the history of law from antiquity to the present. The survey is composed of four sections: *Droits de l'antiquité* (subdivided by ancient civilization), *Droit romain médiéval, Histoire du droit canonique, Histoire générale du droit et des institutions.* Also included are annotated tables of contents of periodicals devoted to legal history, lists of dissertations, various regional *chroniques*, and reports of societies. Each of the major sections appears at least once a year. Signed or initialed descriptive or critical annotations (up to 250 words).

Examined: ser. 4, vol. 44 (1966), bibliography for 1964–65, *ca.* 500 items.

*185. Traditio: Studies in Ancient and Medieval History, Thought and Religion. New York. 1943– . Annual.

Each volume contains the "Bulletin of the Institute of Medieval Canon Law," which includes a select bibliography of articles and books published during a given period in Europe and North America concerning all aspects, theoretical, practical, and textual, of medieval canon law. The publications are listed alphabetically by author. Frequent descriptive or critical annotations (up to 100 words). The bibliography began in 1956.

Examined: vol. 22 (1966), bibliography for 1965–66, 232 items.

See also:
7. **Deutsches Archiv für Erforschung des Mittelalters**
10. **International Bibliography of Historical Sciences**
140. **Répertoire général de sciences religieuses**
141. **Revue d'histoire ecclésiastique: Bibliographie**
145. **Ostkirchliche Studien**
216. **Elenchus bibliographicus**

D. Sociology, Anthropology, and Folklore

186. **Annales de démographie historique:** Études et chronique.
(Société de démographie historique.) Paris. 1964– .
Annual.
    Entitled **Études et chronique de démographie historique,**
1964.

Each annual volume contains a bibliography of articles and
books recently published in Europe and North America concerning the historical demography of Europe from antiquity
to the present. The publications are classified according to general studies, antiquity, the Middle Ages, France (arranged by
region), Europe (arranged by country), and other continents.
Descriptive annotations (up to 250 words). Titles normally are
also given in French. Reviews are noted.
    Examined: vol. 2 (1965), bibliography for 1959–64, *ca.* 350
items.

187. **Arts et traditions populaires.** (Société d'ethnographie
française.) Paris. 1953– . Three issues yearly.
    Continues bibliography in **Le mois d'ethnographie fran-
çaise.** (Société d'ethnographie française.) Paris. 1947–52.

The last issue of each annual volume normally contains the
"Bibliographie d'ethnologie française," which includes articles
and books published in France during a given period concerning
French ethnography, including agriculture, folklore, technology,
art, and culture. Classified by topic. Occasional descriptive annotations (up to 100 words). Reviews are noted.
    Examined: vol. 13 (1965), bibliography for 1963–64, 1,071
items.

188. Bulletin signalétique 21: Sociologie, ethnologie. (Centre national de la recherche scientifique.) Paris. 1947– . Quarterly.

An extensive bibliography of articles recently published throughout the world concerning sociology and ethnology. The publications are classified within two major sections, sociology and ethnology, which are extensively subdivided by topic, e.g. *Méthodes et techniques de recherche; Sociologie et histoire; Systèmes sociaux et civilisations; Sociologie juridique et morale; Sociologie des religions; Théories, méthodes, documents; Ethnologie historique; Structures sociales et politiques; Lieux et objets de culte; Vie religieuse.* Descriptive annotations (up to 150 words). This bibliography appears as a separate publication and also as section 21 of the **Bulletin signalétique (5)**. Annual author and subject indexes.

Examined: vol. 20 (1966), bibliography for 1964–65, 4,325 items, *ca.* 2,500 serials indexed (for sections 19–24 of the **Bulletin**).

189. International Bibliography of Social and Cultural Anthropology. Bibliographie internationale d'anthropologie sociale et culturelle. (International Committee for Social Sciences Documentation.) London and Chicago. 1955– (publ. 1958–). Annual.
    Part of **International Bibliography of the Social Sciences. Bibliographie internationale des sciences sociales.**

An extensive bibliography of articles and books published during a given year throughout the world concerning social and cultural anthropology. The publications are classified within ten major divisions: *Anthropology: General Studies; Material and Methods of Anthropology; Morphological Foundations; General Ethnographic Studies of Peoples and Communities; Social Organization and Relationships; Religion, Magic and Witchcraft; Problems of Knowledge, Arts and Science, Folk Traditions; Studies of Culture and Personality, "National Character"; Problems of Acculturation and Social Change, Contact Situations; Applied Anthropology.* The focus of the bibliography is on non-European societies. Brief descriptive annotations. Reviews are noted. Author and subject indexes.

Examined: vol. 10 (1964, publ. 1966), bibliography for 1964, 3,708 items, *ca.* 1,500 serials indexed.

190. International Bibliography of Sociology. Bibliographie internationale de sociologie. (International Committee for Social Sciences Documentation.) London and Chicago. 1951– (publ. 1952–). Annual.

Part of **International Bibliography of the Social Sciences. Bibliographie internationale des sciences sociales.**

Published 1952–55 in **Current Sociology. La sociologie contemporaine.** (International Sociological Association.) Paris.

An extensive bibliography of articles and books published during a given year throughout the world concerning all aspects of sociology. The publications are classified by topic under six major headings: *History and Organization of Social Studies, Theories and Methods of Sociology, Social Structure, Social Control and Communication, Social Change, Social Problems and Social Policy.* While the emphasis of the bibliography is decidedly modern, there is some material on medieval religious institutions, technology, and social stratification. Brief descriptive annotations. Reviews are noted. Author and subject indexes.

Examined: vol. 14 (1964, publ. 1966), bibliography for 1964, 5,050 items, *ca.* 1,500 serials indexed.

191. Internationale volkskundliche Bibliographie. International Folklore Bibliography. Bibliographie internationale des arts et traditions populaires. (Société internationale d'ethnologie et de folklore.) Bonn. 1939– (publ. 1949–). Biennial.

Continues **Volkskundliche Bibliographie.** (Verband deutscher Vereine für Volkskunde.) Berlin. 1917–38.

Each volume comprises an extensive bibliography of articles and books published throughout the world during a given period concerning the historical folklore of the peoples of greater Europe. Publications are classified by topic within twenty-two major subject divisions, including *Technology, Arts and Crafts, Industries; Manners and Customs, Festivals, Pastimes; Social Traditions, Folk Law; Popular Beliefs* (e.g. veneration of the saints, pilgrimages, and witches and magicians); '*Maer-*

chen,' Folk-Tales, Myths, Legends. Occasional brief descriptive annotations. Author and subject indexes. Examined: 1961–62 (publ. 1965), bibliography for 1961–62, 8,927 items, *ca.* 1,500 serials indexed.

192. Southern Folklore Quarterly. (University of Florida, Gainesville. South Atlantic Modern Language Association.) Jacksonville. 1937– . Quarterly.

The first number of each annual volume comprises a bibliography of articles and books published throughout the world during the previous year concerning the folklore of the past and present. Publications are arranged alphabetically by author within ten major subject divisions: *General Folklore; Prose Narrative; Song, Game, Dance; Drama; Ritual, Festival; Belief and Practice; Material Culture; Speech; Proverb; Riddle.* Descriptive annotations (up to 100 words). Author index. Bibliography began in 1938.
Examined: vol. 29 (1965), bibliography for 1964, 878 items.

See also:
10. International Bibliography of Historical Sciences

VIII. Intellectual History

A. Biblical Studies and Exegesis

*193. Bulletin de la Bible latine. (Abbaye de Maredsous.) Maredsous. 1960– . Irregular.
Published as a separately paginated supplement in **Revue bénédictine.** (Abbaye de Maredsous.) Maredsous.
Continues **Bulletin d'ancienne littérature chrétienne latine.** (Abbaye de Maredsous.) Maredsous. Published 1921–59 in **Revue bénédictine.**

Each volume comprises a bibliography of articles and books published during a given period, principally in Europe and North America, concerning the Latin Bible, namely, the history of the text of the scriptures, biblical exegesis, and biblical iconography in art and literature. The publications are arranged according to the text of the scriptures. Where applicable they are grouped by subject, e.g. *Ensemble de la Bible: Généralités, Manuscrits, Pères, Lexiques.* Frequent descriptive and critical annotations (up to 700 words). Reviews are occasionally noted. The **Bulletin d'ancienne littérature chrétienne latine** published in **Revue bénédictine** was divided into two parts: *Littérature*

94

biblique and *Littérature non-biblique.* The latter part was discontinued with the completion of vol. 4 of the **Bulletin;** the former continues as the present bibliography. Indexes at the end of each volume for annotated publications, biblical manuscripts and texts, patristic authors and texts, and major words. Examined: vol. 5 (1964–), bibliography for 1960– , 505 items through 1968.

*194. Elenchus bibliographicus biblicus. (Pontificium institutum biblicum.) Roma. 1923– . Annual.

Published as a separately paginated supplement in **Biblica:** Commentarii ad rem biblicam scientifice investigandam. (Pontificium institutum biblicum.) Roma. Continues bibliography in **Biblica,** 1920–22.

Each annual volume comprises an extensive bibliography of articles and books recently published, principally in Europe and North America, concerning biblical studies and exegesis. The publications are classified by topic within several general areas: introduction to biblical study, history of the text, works on individual books of the scriptures, biblical history and theology. Occasional brief descriptive annotations. Reviews are noted. Index of authors, subjects, and words from the ancient tongues. A supplement, **Elenchus suppletorius (195),** is published in **Verbum Domini.**

Examined: vol. 45 (1964), bibliography for 1963–64, 4,197 items, *ca.* 500 serials indexed.

195. Elenchus suppletorius. (Pontificium institutum biblicum.) Roma. 1960– . Irregular.

Published periodically as a separately paginated supplement in **Verbum Domini:** Commentarii de re biblica. (Pontificium institutum biblicum.) Roma.

This bibliography is a supplement to **Elenchus bibliographicus biblicus (194).** It contains publications of a more general or practical nature along with works omitted from the larger bibliography, such as reviews of books previously listed, recent publications, or items accidentally omitted. It also adds a new section, *Hermeneutica practica et actio biblica,* which contains publications concerning the intellectual, instructional, liturgical, pastoral, and spiritual impact of the Bible in contemporary society. With these exceptions, the scope, format, subject organization, and volume numeration are those of the **Elenchus bibliographicus biblicus.** Annual author and subject index. Examined: vol. 46 (1965), bibliography for 1962–64, 1,035 items.

196. Internationale Zeitschriftenschau für Bibelwissenschaft und Grenzgebiete. International Review of Biblical Studies. Revue internationale des études bibliques. Düsseldorf. 1951– (publ. 1952–). Annual.

Each annual volume comprises an extensive bibliography of articles recently published throughout the world concerning biblical studies and exegesis. The articles are normally classified by topic within fourteen sections: *Text; Auslegung; Biblische Theologie; Bibel in Kult und Gemeinde; Auslegungsgeschichte; Schriften ausserhalb der Bibel; Umwelt der Bibel; Sprache; Geschichte Israels; Biblische Archäologie und Topographie; Judentum, Frühe Kirche, Gnosis; Bibel in Kunst- und Literaturgeschichte; Bibliographie; Nachträge.* The section *Bibliographie* includes monographic publications. Book reviews are listed by reviewer. Initialed descriptive annotations (up to 250 words). Indexes of series and serials surveyed, of authors being reviewed, and of authors. Examined: vol. 12 (1965–66, publ. 1966) bibliography for 1965–66, 2,210 items, *ca.* 300 serials indexed.

197. New Testament Abstracts: A Record of Current Periodical Literature. (Theological Faculty of Weston College.) Weston, Massachusetts. 1956– . Three issues yearly.

Each issue comprises a bibliography of book reviews, articles, and books recently published throughout the world concerning New Testament studies. The abstracts are arranged in three groups: abstracts of articles, abstracts of book reviews, and notices of new books. Each group is subdivided by New Testament book and by topic. Abstracts of up to 300 words. Annual indexes of principal scriptural texts, authors and reviewers, book reviews, and book notices. Examined: vol. 10 (1965–66), bibliography for 1965–66,

1,050 articles and book reviews, *ca.* 450 new books, *ca.* 250 journals abstracted.

198. Revue biblique. (École pratique d'études bibliques.) Paris. 1892– . Quarterly.

Each issue contains a bibliographic survey of articles and books recently published in Europe and North America concerning biblical studies. The survey is divided into several sections, each covering a topic such as *Ancien Testament, Saint Paul, Origines chrétiennes.* Publications devoted to the text of the scriptures and to biblical exegesis in the medieval period are included. Signed or initialed descriptive or critical annotations of up to 750 words accompany most items. Annual author and subject index.
Examined: vol. 71 (1964), bibliography for 1962–63, *ca.* 350 items.

See also:
139. International Bibliography of the History of Religions
140. Répertoire général de sciences religieuses
141. Revue d'histoire ecclésiastique: Bibliographie
142. Zeitschrift für die neutestamentliche Wissenschaft und die Kunde der älteren Kirche
216. Elenchus bibliographicus

B. Liturgy and Hagiography

199. Analecta bollandiana. (Société des Bollandistes.) Bruxelles. 1882– . Semiannual.

Each issue contains the "Bulletin des publications hagiographiques," which is primarily a list of books recently published in Europe and North America concerning hagiography and aids to hagiographical research. Signed critical reviews (up to 2,000 words). Annual indexes of saints and authors. Bibliography began in 1891.
Examined: vol. 84 (1966), bibliography for 1965–66, 47 books.

*200. Archiv für Liturgiewissenschaft. (Abt-Herwegen-Institut für liturgische und monastische Forschung, Abtei Maria Laach.) Regensburg. 1950– . Annual.

Continues bibliography in **Jahrbuch für Liturgiewissenschaft.** (Verein zur Pflege der Liturgiewissenschaft, Abtei Maria Laach.) Münster. 1921–35 (publ. 1921–41).

In each issue, the section "Literaturbericht" contains a series of signed bibliographic reports on articles and books published during a given period, principally in Europe and North America, concerning a particular aspect of liturgical studies (e.g. *Liturgie und Kunst, Gregorianischer Gesang, Monastische Liturgie*). The subjects vary from year to year. Within the report, the publications are classified by topic. A number of recent publications concerning liturgical studies are listed at the conclusion of each issue. Descriptive or critical annotations (up to 3,500 words). Biennial indexes of authors, biblical texts, patristic and medieval texts, words and subjects.

Examined: vol. 8 (1963–64), bibliography for 1960–63, 7 reports, 816 items, *ca.* 125 serials indexed.

201. Ephemerides mariologicae: Commentarii de re mariali a superioribus scholis Congregationis missionariorum filiorum exarati. Madrid. 1951– . Three issues yearly.

The last number of each annual volume contains the "Ephemeridum mariologicus prospectus," a bibliography of articles published during the previous year in Europe and the western hemisphere concerning mariology. Publications are classified by topic and historical period. Occasional brief descriptive annotations.

Examined: vol. 17 (1967), bibliography for 1966, *ca.* 200 items.

202. Jahrbuch für Liturgik und Hymnologie. (Internationale Arbeitsgemeinschaft für Hymnologie.) Kassel. 1955– . Annual.

Each annual volume contains two bibliographies, "Literaturbericht zur Liturgik" and "Literaturbericht zur Hymnologie," which survey articles and books recently published in Europe and North America concerning the origins and development of Christian liturgy and hymnology, respectively. The first bibliography is divided into *Die Liturgieforschung in Deutschland* (subdivided into *Die Bibel, Geschichte des Predigt- und Abend-*

mahlsgottesdienstes, Die Predigt, Taufe im Urchristentum, Kalendar und Perikopenfragen, Christliche Archäologie) and *Die Liturgieforschung in den fremdsprachigen Ländern* (subdivided by country). The second bibliography is divided into *Theologie und Musik, Hymnologie, Kirchenmusik, Allgemeine Musikgeschichte,* and *Hymnologische Forschung in fremdsprachigen Ländern* (subdivided by country). Frequent descriptive or critical annotations (up to 500 words) in each bibliography. Indexes of liturgical phrases and of names.
Examined: vol. 11 (1966, publ. 1967), bibliographies for 1964, *ca.* 800 items.

203. Les questions liturgiques et paroissiales. (Abbaye du Mont César.) Louvain. 1910– . Quarterly.

Each number contains one installment of the annual "Bulletin de littérature liturgique," which comprises a bibliography of articles and books recently published, principally in Europe and North America, concerning liturgical and pastoral questions. The focus of the bibliography is on current liturgical practice. The publications are classified by topic. Frequent descriptive annotations (up to 250 words). Annual author index.
Examined: vol. 46 (1965), bibliography for 1963–64, 1,331 items.

204. Yearbook of Liturgical Studies. Notre Dame, Indiana. 1960– . Annual.

Each annual volume contains a bibliography of articles recently published, principally in Europe and North America, concerning the historical development of the liturgy and current liturgical practice. Classified by topic. Frequent descriptive annotations (up to 500 words). Author and subject index.
Examined: vol. 4 (1963), bibliography for 1962, 1,078 items.

See also:
140. **Répertoire général de sciences religieuses**
141. **Revue d'histoire ecclésiastique: Bibliographie**
145. **Ostkirchliche Studien**
Section X, Music

C. Pedagogy

205. Bulletin signalétique 20: Psychologie, pédagogie. (Centre national de la recherche scientifique.) Paris. 1947– . Quarterly.

An extensive bibliography of articles recently published throughout the world concerning psychology and pedagogy. The publications are classified by topic within three major sections: psychology, abnormal psychology, and pedagogy. The section on pedagogy contains material on the history and philosophy of education, although it is primarily modern in emphasis. Descriptive annotations (up to 150 words). This bibliography appears as a separate publication and also as section 20 of the **Bulletin signalétique (5).** Annual author and subject indexes. Separate index of psychological concepts.

Examined: vol. 20 (1966), bibliography for 1964–65, 8,398 items, *ca.* 2,500 serials indexed (for sections 19–24 of the **Bulletin**).

206. Paedagogica historica: International Journal of the History of Education. Revue internationale d'histoire de la pédagogie. (Centre for the Study of the History of Education, University of Ghent.) Gent. 1961– . Semiannual.

Each issue contains the "Index bibliographicus Gandensis," a list of current acquisitions of the Centre for the Study of the History of Education at the University of Ghent. It comprises a bibliography of articles and books recently published throughout the world concerning the history, theory, and practice of education from antiquity to the present. Publications are classified by topic, historical period, or geographic region under five major headings: *Généralités; Études d'ensemble; Histoire par époque, Vie et oeuvre des pédagogues; Histoire comparée, histoire nationale et locale; Monographies historiques.* Occasional brief descriptive annotations. This journal also contains a list of dissertations in two parts, one classified by subject, the other devoted to a specific topic which varies with each issue.

Examined: vol. 5 (1965), bibliography for 1963–65, *ca.* 1,750 items.

D. Theology and Philosophy

207. Augustiniana: Tijdschrift voor de Studie van Sint Augustinus en de Augustijnenorde. Revue pour l'étude de Saint Augustin et de l'ordre des Augustins. (Institutum historicum augustinianum Lovanii.) Louvain. 1951– . Semiannual.

Each annual volume normally contains the "Répertoire bibliographique de Saint Augustin," which includes articles and books recently published in Europe and North America concerning the life, writings, and influence of St. Augustine. The publications are classified by topic under seven major headings: *Bibliographies et bulletins, Vie et personne, Oeuvres, Doctrine, Sources et relations, Influence et survie, Afrique du Nord.* The sections on Augustine's works and theology are particularly extensive. Book reviews are noted. Reviews for items included in previous bibliographies are listed in a separate section. Frequent brief descriptive annotations. The bibliography was cumulated as **Répertoire bibliographique de Saint Augustin, 1950–60.** T. van Bavel, ed. Steenbergen. 1963. This journal also publishes the "Bibliographie d'histoire augustinienne" **(149).**

Examined: vol. 10 (1960), bibliography for 1958–59, 462 items.

208. Bibliografia filosofica italiana. (Centro di studi filosofici di Gallarate.) Brescia. 1949– (publ. 1950–). Annual.
Continues **Bibliografia filosofica italiana dal 1900 al 1950.** (Istituto di studi filosofici. Centro nazionale di informazioni bibliografiche. Centro di studi filosofici cristiani di Gallarate.) 4 vols. Roma. 1950–56.

Each annual volume comprises a bibliography of articles and books recently published in Italy or reviewed in Italian journals concerning primarily Western philosophy. The publications are classified into five major sections: *Bibliografie, dizionari, enciclopedie; Congressi, miscellanee, rassegne; Edizioni di testi* (subdivided by historical period); *Storia della filosofia* (subdivided by historical period); *Filosofia* (subdivided by philosophical subject). Reviews in Italian journals are noted. Index of authors and reviewers.

Examined: 1965 (publ. 1966), bibliography for 1966, 1,854 items, *ca.* 100 serials indexed.

209. Bibliografisch Repertorium. Louvain. 1939–   . Quarterly. Supplement to **Tijdschrift voor Filosofie.** Louvain.

This is the same bibliography as **Répertoire bibliographique de la philosophie (220).**

*****210. Bibliographia patristica:** Internationale patristische Bibliographie. W. Schneemelcher, ed. (Patristische Kommission der Akademien der Wissenschaften zu Göttingen, Heidelberg, München.) Berlin. 1956–   (publ. 1959–   ). Annual.

A bibliography of articles and books published throughout the world during a given year concerning the thought and writings of the Patristic Age (to 787 in the East and 667 in the West). The publications are classified by topic under nine major headings: *Generalia; Novum Testamentum atque Apocrypha; Auctores; Liturgica; Iuridica, symbola; Doctrina auctorum et historia dogmatum; Gnostica; Patrum exegesis Veteris et Novi Testamenti; Recensiones.* In the last section, book reviews are listed by author being reviewed. Author index.

Examined: vol. 9 (1964, publ. 1967), bibliography for 1964, 1,470 items, 430 reviews, *ca.* 1,000 serials indexed.

211. Bibliographie de la philosophie. Bibliography of Philosophy. (Institut international de philosophie.) Paris. 1954–   . Quarterly.

Continues **Bibliographie de la philosophie.** (Institut international de philosophie.) Paris. 1937–53 (publ. 1937–58). And "Bibliography of Philosophy" published 1934–37 in **The Journal of Philosophy.** Baltimore.

An extensive bibliography of books recently published throughout the world concerning philosophy, its history and problems. The publications are classified under the following headings: *Philosophy in General* . . . , *Logic* . . . , *Philosophical Psychology, Philosophy of Art* . . . , *Philosophy of Value* . . . , *Social Philosophy* . . . , *Philosophy of History* . . . , *Philosophy of Religion, History of Philosophy, Reference Books.* . . . Descriptive or critical annotations (up to 300 words). Annual indexes of books, names, and publishers.

Examined: vol. 12 (1965), bibliography for 1963–64, 1,687 items.

*212. Bulletin de philosophie médiévale. (Société internationale pour l'étude de la philosophie médiévale.) Louvain. 1959– . Annual.
    Entitled **Bulletin de la Société internationale pour l'étude de la philosophie médiévale,** 1959–63.

Each annual volume contains a variety of bibliographic media which attempt to survey current developments in the study of medieval philosophy throughout the world, with emphasis on work done by European scholars. The articles appear under the following headings: I. *Notices sur les institutions ou associations adonnées spécialement à l'étude de la pensée médiévale* (lists institutions by country), II. *Renseignements concernant les éditions et les travaux en cours* (in four groups: lists of authors and addresses, studies relative to medieval authors, studies of specific doctrines and themes, and editions of medieval texts), III. *Informations diverses* (bibliographies, articles concerning bibliographic problems; among these is a regular list of doctoral dissertations concerning medieval philosophy arranged by country), IV. *Chroniques nationales* (news of activities in various medieval institutes), V. *Questions posées par les chercheurs,* and VI. *Informations concernant la S.I.E.P.M.* (reports, statutes, lists of members and addresses, works published by members or sent to the society during the previous year). Index of ancient and medieval authors; index to vols. 1–3 in vol. 3 (1961).
    Examined: vol. 6 (1964, publ. 1965), bibliography for 1964, II. 393 items, III. 105 dissertations, VI. 110 titles received.

*213. Bulletin de théologie ancienne et médiévale. (Abbaye du Mont César.) Louvain. 1929– . Semiannual.
    Published as a supplement to **Recherches de théologie ancienne et médiévale.** (Abbaye du Mont César.) Louvain.

Each issue comprises a bibliography of articles and books recently published, principally in Europe and North America, concerning the history, development, and interpretation of Christian theology from its beginnings to the later Middle Ages. Publications are listed in chronological order of their contents. Initialed descriptive or critical annotations (up to 600 words). Author index. Extensive quadrennial indexes of names, doctrines, and manuscripts. These also constitute indexes to the contents of the publications themselves in so far as they are represented by the annotations.

Examined: vol. 9 (1962–65), bibliography for 1958–65, 2,364 items.

214. Bulletin signalétique 19: Philosophie, sciences religieuses. (Centre national de la recherche scientifique.) Paris. 1947– . Quarterly.

An extensive bibliography of articles recently published throughout the world concerning philosophy and religion. The publications are classified by topic and historical period within eight major sections: *Histoire de la philosophie, Métaphysique et philosophie générale, Théorie des valeurs, Morale, Esthétique, Philosophie de l'histoire et philosophie politique, Logique et philosophie de la connaissance, Sciences religieuses* (including Judaism, Christianity, and Islam). Considerable material concerning medieval ecclesiastical history and theology is included in the last section. Descriptive annotations (up to 150 words). This bibliography appears as a separate publication and also as section 19 of the **Bulletin signalétique (5).** Annual author and subject indexes.

Examined: vol. 20 (1966), bibliography for 1964–65, 7,121 items, *ca.* 2,500 serials indexed (for sections 19–24 of the **Bulletin**).

*215. Bulletin thomiste. (Société thomiste, Le Saulchoir.) Étiolles, par Soisy-sur-Seine. 1924– . Annual.

Published 1924–30 as a separately paginated supplement in **Revue thomiste.** (École de théologie.) Saint-Maximin.

Each issue contains one installment of an extensive triennial bibliography of articles and books recently published throughout the world concerning St. Thomas, his background, and Thomistic thought. The bibliography is divided into seven major sections: *Histoire de S. Thomas, Oeuvres de S. Thomas, Sources doctrinales et littéraires, Doctrines philosophiques, Doctrines théologiques, Histoire du thomisme, Étude de S. Thomas.* Each is subdivided by topic. Signed descriptive or critical annotations (up to 5,000 words). Reviews are noted. Triennial indexes of authors, Thomistic texts, technical terms, manuscripts (Thomistic and other), and reviewers.

Examined: vol. 11 (1960–62, publ. 1962–66) bibliography for 1960–62, 2,330 items.

*216. Elenchus bibliographicus. (Universitas catholica Lovaniensis.) Louvain. 1964–. Semiannual.

Published as a separately paginated supplement in **Ephemerides theologicae Lovanienses:** Commentarii de re theologica et canonica. (Universitas catholica Lovaniensis.) Louvain.

Continues semiannual "Elenchus bibliographicus" in **Ephemerides theologicae Lovanienses,** 1924–63.

Each issue comprises an extensive bibliography of articles and books recently published, primarily in Europe and North America, concerning theology, scriptural exegesis, and canon law. The publications are classified by topic under nine major headings: *Generalia, Historia religionum, Scriptura Sacra Veteris Testamenti, Scriptura Sacra Novi Testamenti, Theologia fundamentalis et apologetica, Dogmatica specialis, Theologia asceticomystica, Theologia moralis, Ius canonicum.* Annual index of names.

Examined: vol. 40 (1964), bibliography for 1963, *ca.* 7,500 items, *ca.* 450 serials indexed.

217. **Estudios eclesiásticos:** Revista trimestral de investigación e información teológica. (Facultades de teología de la Compañía de Jesús en España.) Madrid. 1922– . Quarterly.

The fourth number of each annual volume normally contains the "Literatura eclesiástica española," a bibliography of articles and books published in Spain during a given year concerning the theology and history of the Church Universal. Articles concerning Spanish ecclesiastical history published in foreign journals are also included. The publications are classified by topic within three major sections: *Generalidades de teología, Bíblica, Moral y derecho canónico.* Occasional brief descriptive annotations. Index of names. Bibliography began in 1946.

Examined: vol. 40 (1965), bibliography for 1963, *ca.* 1,250 items.

218. Pensamiento: Revista trimestral de investigación e información filosófica. (Facultades de filosofía de la Compañía de Jesús en España.) Madrid. 1945– . Quarterly.

Each annual volume normally contains a bibliography of articles and books recently published, principally in Spain and Latin America, concerning historical and systematic philosophy. The first section is divided by historical period. In the medieval section, particular attention is paid to Spanish publication on Islamic thought, St. Thomas, and Raymond Lull. The second section is divided by topic. Each issue also contains reviews or descriptive annotations of books and articles. Index of names.

Examined: vol. 21 (1965), bibliography for 1963–64, 874 items.

219. Religious and Theological Abstracts. (Religious and Theological Abstracts, Inc.) Myerstown, Pennsylvania. 1958– . Semiannual.

Each issue comprises a list of abstracts of articles recently published, principally in Europe and North America, concerning theology and the history and practice of the Christian faith, with emphasis on the modern period. The abstracts (up to 300 words) are arranged by topic under four major headings: *Biblical, Theological, Historical,* and *Practical.* Separately published annual subject, author, and scriptural indexes.

Examined: vol. 9 (1966), bibliography for 1964–65, 1,188 items, 150 serials abstracted.

*220. Répertoire bibliographique de la philosophie. (Société philosophique de Louvain.) Louvain. 1949– . Quarterly.

Continues **Répertoire bibliographique,** a separately paginated quarterly supplement in **Revue philosophique de Louvain.** (Société philosophique de Louvain.) Louvain. 1934–48.

The first three numbers of each annual volume comprise an extensive bibliography of articles and books recently published in the Catalan, Dutch, English, French, German, Spanish, and

Portuguese languages concerning the history and contemporary study of Eastern and Western philosophy from antiquity to the present. Each number is divided into two major sections: *Histoire de la philosophie* (classified by historical period and geographic region) and *Philosophie* (classified by topic). The fourth number contains a bibliography of book reviews in the serials indexed, listed by author being reviewed. Annual indexes of names and of anonyms. This bibliography is also published as **Bibliografisch repertorium (209)**.

Examined: vol. 17 (1965), bibliography for 1963–65, 6,248 items, *ca.* 325 serials indexed.

221. Revue d'ascétique et de mystique. Toulouse. 1920– . Quarterly.

The third number of each annual volume normally contains the "Bibliographie française de spiritualité," which includes articles and books published in the French language during the previous year concerning Christian spirituality. Classified by topic and historical period under three headings: *Instruments de travail, Doctrine spirituelle, Histoire de la spiritualité*. Author index.

Examined: vol. 42 (1966), bibliography for 1965, 784 items.

222. Revue des études augustiniennes. Paris. 1955– . Three issues yearly.

Continues quarterly bibliography published 1949–54 in **L'année théologique augustinienne.** Paris.

One issue of each annual volume contains the "Bulletin augustinien," a bibliography of articles and books published throughout the world during a given year concerning St. Augustine, his writings, and their influence. Classified by topic within six major sections: *Répertoires bibliographiques, Textes, Études critiques, Études générales, Doctrines philosophiques, Doctrines théologiques*. Initialed descriptive or critical annotations (up to 1000 words). Reviews are noted. Annual author index.

Examined: vol. 12 (1966), bibliography for 1964, 432 items.

223. Revue des sciences philosophiques et théologiques. Paris. 1907– . Quarterly.

This journal contains several bibliographic media which survey recent publication in Europe and North America concerning Eastern and Western intellectual history, in particular philosophy and theology, from antiquity to the present. Each number of the **Revue** contains one or more "Bulletins," which are extensive critical surveys (up to 50 pages) of recent publication in their respective areas. The subject organization is unique to each "Bulletin," although they are normally divided into major sections in which each paragraph is devoted to the literature of one specific topic. Those especially pertinent to medieval studies are: "Bulletin d'histoire des doctrines médiévales" (medieval philosophy and theology and their classical and nonclassical sources; published since 1955), "Bulletin Marial" (the history and doctrine of mariology; published since 1962), and "Bulletin d'histoire des doctrines chrétiennes: Antiquité" (ancient and patristic theology and philosophy; published since 1907). In addition, each number of the **Revue** contains (1) "Recensions des revues" (an extensive list of tables of contents of current issues of journals in intellectual history, arranged alphabetically by title, with brief descriptive annotations accompanying the pertinent articles), and (2) "Notices bibliographiques" (signed critical reviews of books in this field). One number of each annual volume contains a list of doctoral dissertations concerning intellectual history presented to the Catholic faculties of French universities during the previous year. The contents of each of these bibliographic media are included in the annual author and subject indexes.

Examined: vol. 48 (1964), bibliography for 1961–63; 669 items in "Bulletins," 36 book reviews, *ca.* 250 journals, 24 dissertations.

224. Scripta recenter edita: Commentarii bibliographici qui, ut bibliothecis theologicis necnon philosophicis bono sint usui, eduntur. (Vereniging voor Seminarie- en Kloosterbibliothecarissen.) Nijmegen. 1959– . Nine issues yearly.

Each issue comprises a bibliography of books recently published, principally in Europe and North America, concerning philosophy and theology. Classified by topic. This bibliography attempts to provide current information about all recently published books that might be of interest to librarians in theology and philosophy.

Occasional brief descriptive annotations. Author indexes appear in each issue and are cumulated annually. Examined: vol. 7 (1965), bibliography for 1964–65, *ca.* 7,500 items.

225. Theología. (Hierà synódos tês ekklesías tês helládos.) Athenai. 1923– . Quarterly.

Each annual volume contains a bibliography of articles and books recently published in Europe, North America, and the Middle East concerning Christian theology, with particular emphasis upon Greek Orthodox theology. The bibliography is divided into two parts: titles published in the Roman alphabet appear in the third number, and titles published in the Greek alphabet appear in the fourth number. In each, the titles are listed alphabetically by author. Until 1962, the items listed were included in the annual Greek and Roman author indexes. The bibliography began in 1948 (for 1940). Examined: vol. 36 (1965), bibliography for 1964, *ca.* 475 Roman items, *ca.* 225 Greek items.

226. Theologische Literaturzeitung: Monatsschrift für das gesamte Gebiet der Theologie und Religionswissenschaft. Leipzig. 1876– . Monthly.

Each monthly issue contains a survey of recent periodical and monographic publications in Europe and North America in the fields of theology and religion. The survey is organized by subject; these vary slightly with each issue but normally include the following: general studies, ancient Near East and Judaica, Old and New Testament, ecclesiastical history (subdivided by chronological period), philosophy, systematic theology, practical theology, liturgy and music. Each subject area normally includes two or three signed critical reviews and a short list of articles in the field. Reports of congresses and dissertations, commemorative essays on the work of individual scholars, select contents of recent journals, and lists of new books appear at irregular intervals. Examined: vol. 91 (1966), bibliography for 1965, *ca.* 550 reviews, *ca.* 1,600 articles, *ca.* 475 new books.

227. Theologische Revue. (Katholische-Theologische Fakultät der Universität Münster.) Münster. 1902– . Bimonthly.

Each number contains a bibliography of articles and books recently published, principally in Europe and North America, concerning theology and church history. Classified by topic or historical period under thirteen headings, the largest of which are *Gesamttheologie, Religionswissenschaft und -geschichte, Bibelwissenschaft, Kirchengeschichte, Fundamentaltheologie und Dogmatik.*
Examined: vol. 63 (1967), bibliography for 1966–67, *ca.* 3,000 items.

See also:
  7. Deutsches Archiv für Erforschung des Mittelalters
  10. International Bibliography of Historical Sciences
  140. Répertoire général de sciences religieuses
  141. Revue d'histoire ecclésiastique: Bibliographie
  145. Ostkirchliche Studien

IX. Literature and Linguistics

A. General

228. Bibliographie linguistique. Linguistic Bibliography. (Comité international permanent des linguistes.) Utrecht and Anvers. 1939–   (publ. 1949–   ). Annual.

Each annual volume comprises an extensive bibliography of articles and books published throughout the world during a given year concerning the study of living and dead languages and dialects. Classified by topic, linguistic group, and language. Occasional brief descriptive annotations. Reviews are noted. Author index.

Examined: 1964 (publ. 1966), bibliography for 1964, 12,254 items, *ca.* 1,000 serials indexed.

229. Bulletin bibliographique de la Société internationale Arthurienne. Bibliographical Bulletin of the International Arthurian Society. (Société internationale Arthurienne.) Paris. 1949–   . Annual.

Each volume contains a bibliography of articles and books published during the previous year, principally in Europe and North America, concerning the Arthurian Cycle, from its origins through the sixteenth century. Publications are arranged by country of publication, each subdivided into *Texts and Translations, Critical and Historical Studies,* and *Reviews.* Descriptive or critical annotations (up to 400 words). Reviews are noted.

111

Indexes of authors (ancient and medieval) and of subjects and works.
Examined: vol. 18 (1966), bibliography for 1965, 278 items.

230. Bulletin signalétique 23: Littérature et arts du spectacle. (Centre national de la recherche scientifique.) Paris. 1947– . Quarterly.
Entitled **Bulletin signalétique 23: Esthétique, archéologie, arts,** 1947–66.

An extensive bibliography of articles recently published throughout the world concerning literature and the visual arts. The publications are classified by topic under the following headings: *Généralités; Littérature comparée; Littérature générale; Poésie; Roman, conte, nouvelle; Correspondance, mémoires, journaux intimes; Critique; Art oratoire; Théâtre; Cinéma.* Broad coverage is given to medieval literature and drama. Descriptive annotations (up to 150 words). This bibliography appears as a separate publication and also as section 23 of the **Bulletin signalétique (5).** Annual author and subject indexes. Publications on art and archaeology, included until the last quarter of 1966, are now published separately as **Bulletin signalétique: Domaines complémentaires (124).**
Examined: vol. 20 (1966), bibliography for 1964–65, 8,307 items, *ca.* 2,500 serials indexed (for sections 19–24 of the **Bulletin**).

231. Bulletin signalétique 24: Sciences du langage. (Centre national de la recherche scientifique). Paris. 1947– . Quarterly.
Published in **Bulletin signalétique 21: Sociologie, ethnologie, sciences du langage,** 1956–64.

An extensive bibliography of articles recently published throughout the world concerning all aspects of linguistics and philology. The publications are arranged within a detailed subject classification: *Philosophie du signe et du langage, Physiologie et psychologie du langage, Sociologie du langage, Déterminations spécifiques du langage, Substituts de la parole et communication, Linguistique historique et grammaire comparée, Onomastique, Enseignement des langages, Philologie, Stylistique.* Descriptive annotations (up to 150 words). This bibliography appears as a separate publication and also as section 24 of the **Bulletin signalétique (5).** Annual author and subject indexes.

Examined: vol. 20 (1966), bibliography for 1964–65, 6,413 items, *ca.* 2,500 serials indexed (for sections 19–24 of the **Bulletin).**

*232. **MLA International Bibliography of Books and Articles on the Modern Languages and Literatures.** (Modern Language Association of America.) New York. 1921– (publ. 1922–). Annual.

Entitled **Annual Bibliography,** 1956–62 (publ. 1957–63); **American Bibliography,** 1921–55 (publ. 1922–56).

Reprinted from **PMLA. Publications of the Modern Language Association of America.** New York.

Each annual volume comprises an extensive bibliography of articles and books published throughout the world during a given year concerning the languages and literatures of Europe and the western hemisphere from the Middle Ages to the present. Studies devoted to medieval Latin are also included. The publications are classified by language, subdivided by topic, historical period, and individual literary figure. Author index (beginning with the volume for 1964). The bibliography became international in coverage beginning with the volume for 1956.

Examined: 1965 (publ. 1966), bibliography for 1965, 18,852 items, *ca.* 1,200 serials indexed.

*233. **Onoma:** Bibliographical and Information Bulletin. Bulletin d'information et de bibliographie. (International Centre of Onomastics.) Louvain. 1950– . Three issues biennially.

One number of each volume contains a bibliography in three parts. The first and most important, "Bibliographia onomastica," comprises a series of signed bibliographies of articles and books published throughout the world during a given year concerning onomastics in general, with specific emphasis on Europe. Each individual bibliography lists the publications concerning a given country or continent under three headings: *Bio-bibliography, Toponomy,* and *Anthroponomy.* Occasional brief descriptive annotations (up to 100 words). Reviews are noted. Part II contains a collection of tables of contents of current issues of European and North American onomastic journals. Part III comprises a select bibliography of current publications, excluding articles, which are classified by the period, country, or continent to which they pertain, with sections devoted to generalia and linguistics. Books donated by their authors receive brief descriptive annotations. These publications will be included in Part I of the following bibliography. Each biennial volume frequently has an "Annex" which contains addenda to Parts II and III. The journal at times contains lists of dissertations and separately paginated special bibliographies concerning specific topics or geographic areas.

Examined: vol. 10 (1962–63, publ. 1963–64), Part I, bibliography for 1960, ca. 2,750 items; Part II, bibliography for 1961, 18 journals, Annex for 1963, 10 journals; Part III, bibliography for 1961, ca. 175 items, Annex for 1963–64, 432 items.

234. **Studier i modern språkvetenskap:** Acta Universitatis Stockholmiensis. **Stockholm Studies in Modern Philology.** (Nyfilologiska sällskapet i Stockholm.) Stockholm. 1898– . Irregular.

Each volume contains a bibliography of articles and books published during a given period by Swedish authors concerning modern philology. The material is listed by author in three sections — *Romance, English*, and *German Philology* — each followed by a section containing additions to previous bibliographies. Reviews are noted and also listed by reviewer.

Examined: ser. 2, vol. 2 (1964), bibliography for 1959–62, ca. 500 items.

235. **Studies in Philology.** (University of North Carolina.) Chapel Hill, North Carolina. 1906– . Five issues yearly.

One number of each annual volume comprises an extensive bibliography, "Literature of the Renaissance," which contains articles and books published during the previous year in Europe and North America concerning the vernacular and Latin literature of the Renaissance (*ca.* 1400–1650). Classified by vernacular language, subdivided into general works, history, literary forms, and individual authors. Occasional brief descriptive annotations. Reviews are noted. Index of names. The bibliography began in 1922, but was devoted primarily to literature of the English Renaissance until 1938.

Examined: vol. 63 (1966), bibliography for 1965, 3,511 items.

236. Yearbook of Comparative and General Literature. (Comparative Literature Committee, Indiana University.) Bloomington, Indiana. 1952– . Annual.

Continues **Bibliography of Comparative Literature.** F. Baldensperger and W. P. Friederich, eds. Chapel Hill, North Carolina. 1950.

Each annual volume contains an extensive bibliography of articles and books published throughout the world during the previous year concerning the comparative study of the ancient, medieval, and modern literatures of the world. Publications are classified within eight sections (normally corresponding to sections in Baldensperger and Friederich); *Comparative, World and General Literature; Translations, Translators, Correspondents, Travellers, and Other Intermediaries; Themes and Motifs; Literary Genres, Types, Forms and Techniques; Epochs, Currents, and Movements; Bible, Classical Antiquity, Arab Influences, Larger Geographical and Linguistic Units; Individual Countries; Individual Authors.* Occasional brief descriptive annotations. Beginning in 1961, each volume has also included a bibliography of English translations of foreign literature, published during the previous year in the United States. The translations are arranged by original language, including Old English, French, German, Greek, Latin, and Arabic.

Examined: vol. 15 (1966), bibliography for 1965, *ca.* 2,000 items, *ca.* 475 translations.

237. The Year's Work in Modern Language Studies. (Modern Humanities Research Association.) Cambridge. 1929– (publ. 1931–). Annual.

Each annual volume comprises a series of signed bibliographic essays discussing articles and books published throughout the world during a given year concerning the linguistic and literary study of medieval Latin and of the Romance, Germanic, and Slavonic languages from their medieval origins to the present. Each essay covers a given historical period of a language and its literature and is subdivided by topic. Author and subject index.

Examined: vol. 27 (1965, publ. 1966), bibliography for 1965, 59 essays.

See also:
   141. Revue d'histoire ecclésiastique: Bibliographie

B. Germanic Languages

238. Abstracts of English Studies. (National Council of Teachers of English.) Boulder, Colorado. 1958– . Ten issues yearly.

Each issue comprises a bibliography of articles recently published throughout the world concerning the English language and English and American literature. The articles, with signed abstracts of up to 175 words, are listed alphabetically by serial title. Author and subject index in each issue. Annual cumulative indexes of journals abstracted and of authors and subjects.

Examined: vol. 9 (1965), bibliography for 1965, 3,553 articles, *ca.* 325 serials abstracted.

239. Acta philologica Scandinavica: Tidsskrift for nordisk sprogforskning. København. 1926– . Semiannual.

The second issue of each annual volume comprises one installment of the "Bibliography of Scandinavian Philology," which includes articles and books published in Scandinavia during a given period concerning philology and linguistics in general, or published in Europe and North America concerning Scandinavian philology and linguistics. Classified by topic: *General Treatment; Bibliography and Biography; Special Linguistic Branches; Grammar; Linguistic Investigations of Texts; Lexicography; Texts; Translations; Palaeography, Orthography, and Punctuation.* Frequent English summaries (up to 500 words). Book reviews are listed at the end of each section by the author being reviewed. The last installment contains supplements to all topics. Extensive author, subject, and word indexes in the last installment.

Examined: vols. 25–26 (1964), bibliography for 1956–60, 2,088 items, index not yet published.

240. American Speech: A Quarterly of Linguistic Usage. Baltimore. 1925– . Quarterly.

Numbers two and four each contain a brief bibliography entitled "General and Historical Studies," which surveys articles and books recently published in Europe and North America concerning, particularly, English toponomy and Middle English philology. It appears in addition to the regular quarterly bibliography, "Present-Day English." Publications are listed alphabetically by author. Frequent brief descriptive annotations. Reviews are noted. Annual author index. Bibliography began in 1933.

Examined: vol. 40 (1965), bibliography for 1964–65, 84 items.

*241. Annual Bibliography of English Language and Literature. (Modern Humanities Research Association.) Cambridge. 1920– (publ. 1921–). Annual.

An extensive bibliography of articles and books published during a given year in Europe and North America concerning English literature and linguistics from their origins to the present. Linguistic and literary studies are classified by topic and by historical period. Reviews are noted. Subject and author index.

Examined: vol. 39 (1964, publ. 1966), bibliography for 1964, 9,040 items, *ca.* 250 serials indexed.

*242. Bibliographie der deutschen Literaturwissenschaft. C. Köttelwesch, ed. Frankfurt am Main. 1945– (publ. 1957–). Biennial.

An extensive bibliography of articles and books published during a given period, principally in Europe and North America, concerning the history and study of German literature from its beginnings to the present. Classified by topic and historical period. Reviews are noted. Author and subject indexes.

Examined: vol. 6 (1963–64, publ. 1965), bibliography for 1963–64, *ca.* 5,000 items, *ca.* 500 serials indexed.

*243. Bibliography of Old Norse-Icelandic Studies. København. 1963–   (publ. 1964–   ). Annual.

A bibliography of articles and books published during a given year, principally in Europe and North America, concerning "Old Norse language and literature, mediaeval Icelandic and Norwegian civilization, [and] related subjects." Publications are listed alphabetically by author. Occasional brief descriptive annotations. Reviews are noted. Subject index.

Examined: 1965 (publ. 1966), bibliography for 1965, 536 items, *ca.* 100 serials indexed.

*244. Germanistik: Internationales Referatenorgan mit bibliographischen Hinweisen. Tübingen. 1960–   . Quarterly.

Each issue comprises an extensive bibliography of articles and books recently published, primarily in Europe and North America, concerning the study of Germanic languages and literature from their origins to the present. Publications are classified by language, literary form, and historical period. Signed critical annotations (up to 750 words) for monographic publications. Annual index of names.

Examined: vol. 7 (1966), bibliography for 1964–65, 2,953 items, *ca.* 200 serials indexed.

245. Handelingen van de Koninklijke Commissie voor Toponymie & Dialectologie. Bulletin de la Commission royale de toponymie & dialectologie. (Koninklijke Commissie voor Toponymie & Dialectologie.) Bruxelles. 1927–   . Annual.

This journal publishes, at irregular intervals, three bibliographies which report articles and books published during a given period, primarily in Europe, concerning Flemish philology, place-names, and family names.

"De Nederlandse Taalkunde" (formerly "De Nederlandsche Dialectstudie"). A detailed survey of publications concerning Flemish philology. The bibliography is divided into six sections: bibliography and biography; general studies, foreign language and miscellaneous studies; grammatical studies; lexicography; linguistic geography; texts and textual interpretation. Frequent descriptive annotations (up to 100 words). Reviews are noted. Author index.

Examined: vol. 33 (1959), bibliography for 1958, 369 items.

"De Plaatsnamenstudie." A detailed survey of publications concerning the study of Flemish, and to a lesser degree European, place-names. The publications are arranged by geographic region and topic: French Flanders, Northern Netherlands, Frisia, German linguistic areas, English linguistic areas, Scandinavian toponymy, general studies, special studies, Antwerp and Brabant, Limburg and Liège, East and West Flanders, spelling of place-names in the Low Countries, historical and geographic aids, linguistic boundaries and colonization. Frequent descriptive annotations (up to 100 words). Reviews are noted. The bibliography in vol. 1 (1927) covers from the early nineteenth century to 1926.

Examined: vol. 33 (1959), bibliography for 1957–58, *ca.* 400 items.

"De Persoonsnamenstudie." A detailed survey of publications concerning the study of Flemish, and to a lesser degree western European, family names. The publications are listed by broad topic: family histories, romance family names, German family names, English family names, Scandinavian family names. Frequent descriptive annotations. Reviews are noted. Bibliography began in 1942.

Examined: vol. 37 (1963), bibliography for 1959–61, *ca.* 250 items.

This journal also publishes "La philologie wallonne" **(259).**

246. Íslenzk tunga: Tímarit um íslenzka og almenna málfraeði. **Lingua Islandica.** Reykjavík. 1959– . Annual.

Each issue normally contains a bibliography of articles and books published in Europe and North America during a given period concerning Icelandic philology and linguistics. The publications are classified according to linguistic topic, e.g. phonology, grammar, syntax, etymology, onomastics, texts, and sagas. The bibliography began in 1960.

Examined: vol. 6 (1965), bibliography for 1963–64, 185 items, *ca.* 50 serials indexed.

*247. Jahresbericht für deutsche Sprache und Literatur. (Institut für deutsche Sprache und Literatur, Deutsche Akademie der Wissenschaften zu Berlin.) Berlin. 1940– (publ. 1960–   ). Irregular. Continues **Jahresbericht über die Erscheinungen auf dem Gebiete der germanischen Philologie.** (Gesellschaft für deutsche Philologie.) Berlin. 1879–1939 (publ. 1880–1956). And **Jahresbericht über die wissenschaftlichen Erscheinungen auf dem Gebiete der neuern deutschen Literatur.** (Literaturarchiv Gesellschaft.) Berlin. 1890–1939 (publ. 1892–1956).

Each volume comprises an extensive bibliography of articles and books published during a given period, principally in Germany, concerning German linguistics and literature from the origins of the Germanic languages to the present. The publications are classified in four major sections: *Allgemeiner Teil; Sprachlicher Teil* (subdivided into *Indogermanisch, Gotisch, Deutsch, Althochdeutsch,* etc.); *Literaturwissenschaftlicher Teil* (subdivided into *Germanische Kultur und Dichtung, Althochdeutsche Literatur, Mittellateinische Literatur in Deutschland,* etc.); and, in vol. 1 only, *Ergänzungen* (subdivided into *Friesische Sprache und Literatur* and *Niederländische Sprache und Literatur.* Occasional brief descriptive annotations. Reviews are noted. Indexes of authors, subjects, and words. The medieval portions of this bibliography are continued from the **Jahresbericht . . . der germanischen Philologie.**

Examined: vol. 2 (1946–50, publ. 1966), bibliography for 1946–50, 18,240 items, *ca.* 550 serials indexed.

248. Scandinavian Studies. (Society for the Advancement of Scandinavian Study.) Lawrence, Kansas. 1911–   . Quarterly.

One number of each annual volume contains the "American Scandinavian Bibliography," which includes articles and books published during the previous year by American authors in America or in Europe concerning the literature and history of Scandinavia and its peoples. The publications are classified by general subject, subdivided by country (including Iceland and the

Faeroes). Reviews in American journals are noted. Occasional brief descriptive annotations. The bibliography began in 1948. Examined: vol. 36 (1964), bibliography for 1963, 294 items.

249. Svensk litteraturhistorisk bibliografi. (Svenska Litteratursällskapet.) Uppsala. 1880– . Annual. Published as a separately paginated supplement in **Samlaren:** Tidskrift för svensk litteraturhistorisk forskning. (Svensk Litteratursällskapet.) Uppsala. 1880– .

Each annual issue comprises a bibliography of articles and books recently published, primarily in Sweden, concerning the history of Swedish literature. The publications are arranged by subject: *Bibliografi, Allmänt, Religiös litteratur, Tidningsväsen, Folklitteratur, Enskilda författare* (arranged by historical author). Occasional brief descriptive annotations.
Examined: vol. 82 (1963, publ. in **Samlaren** vol. 86, 1965), bibliography for 1963, *ca.* 1,000 items.

250. The Year's Work in English Studies. (English Association.) London. 1919– (publ. 1921–). Annual.

Each annual volume comprises a series of signed bibliographic essays discussing articles and books published throughout the world during a given year concerning the study of English literature and linguistics from their origins to the present. Each essay covers a major historical period or subject, e.g. *Old English Literature, Middle English . . . , Chaucer, The Renaissance.* Author and subject indexes.
Examined: vol. 45 (1964, publ. 1966), bibliography for 1964, 15 essays.

C. Latin Language

*251. **L'année philologique:** Bibliographie critique et analytique de l'Antiquité gréco-latine. (Société internationale de bibliographie classique.) Paris. 1924– (publ. 1928–). Annual.
Continues **Dix années de bibliographie classique:** Bibliographie critique et analytique de l'Antiquité gréco-latine pour la période 1914–24. J. Marouzeau, ed. 2 vols.

Paris. 1927, 1928. And **Bibliographie de l'Antiquité classique, 1896–1914.** S. Lambrino, ed. Vol. 1. Paris. 1951. Vol. 2 in preparation.

A bibliography of articles and books published throughout the world during a given year concerning Greco-Latin antiquity, its origins as well as its afterlife in Byzantium and medieval Europe through the Renaissance. Publications are classified in two sections: *Auteurs et textes*, arranged alphabetically by ancient and medieval author; and *Matières et disciplines*, classified by major cultures and topics under the following headings: *Histoire littéraire; Linguistique et philologie; Histoire des textes; Antiquités; Histoire; Droit; Philosophie; Sciences, techniques, métiers; Les études classiques; Mélanges et recueils*. Occasional descriptive annotations (up to 150 words). Reviews are noted. Indexes of source collections, ancient names, humanists, and modern authors.

Examined: vol. 35 (1964, publ. 1966), bibliography for 1964, *ca.* 12,000 items, *ca.* 600 serials indexed.

252. Bibliographische Beilage. München. 1925– . Quarterly.
Published as a separately paginated supplement in **Gnomon: Kritische Zeitschrift für die gesamte klassische Altertumswissenschaft.** München.

Each issue comprises a bibliography of articles and books recently published primarily in Europe and North America concerning classical culture, including its heritage in patristic, Byzantine, and medieval civilization. The publications are classified by topic.

Examined: vol. 37 (1965), bibliography for 1964–65, *ca.* 3,000 items.

See also:
114. Annuario bibliografico di archeologia

D. Romance Languages

253. L'Alighieri: Rassegna bibliografica dantesca. (Casa di Dante.) Roma. 1960– . Semiannual.

Each issue contains the "Rassegna bibliografica dantesca," which includes articles and books recently published, primarily

in Europe, concerning the writings of Dante and their background and influence. Publications are listed alphabetically by author. Initialed descriptive or critical annotations (up to 500 words).
Examined: vol. 7 (1966), bibliography for 1965, 85 items.

254. Beitræge zur romanischen Philologie. Berlin. 1961– . Semiannual.

Each issue contains half of an annual bibliography of articles and books recently published in the German Democratic Republic, the Soviet Union, and other East European countries concerning romance philology and literature. The publications are classified by topic within eight major sections: general, French, Italian, Rhaeto-Romance, Dalmatian, Spanish, Latin America, Romanian.
Examined: vol. 3 (1964), bibliography for 1960–61, *ca.* 1,500 items.

*255. Bibliographie der französischen Literaturwissenschaft. O. Klapp, ed. Frankfurt am Main. 1956–   (publ. 1960–   ). Biennial.

An extensive bibliography of articles and books published during a given period, principally in Europe and North America, concerning the history and critical study of French literature from its beginnings to the present. Classified by historical period, subdivided by topic and author. Reviews are noted. Author and subject indexes.
Examined: vol. 4 (1963–64, publ. 1965), bibliography for 1963–64, *ca.* 7,500 items, *ca.* 500 serials indexed.

256. Bulletin bibliographique de la Société Rencesvals. (Société Rencesvals pour l'étude des épopées romanes.) Paris. 1958–   . Irregular.

Each issue comprises a bibliography of articles and books recently published, principally in Europe and North America, concerning the medieval romancero and chansons de geste. The publications are classified in two sections: *Textes, éditions, manuscrits, traductions*, and *Études critiques*. Descriptive annotations (up to 500 words). Reviews are listed in a third section, *Comptes*

rendus, by author being reviewed. The journal also contains a list of work in progress and reports on papers presented at recent congresses and colloquia. Indexes of authors (ancient and modern) and subjects (including words).
Examined: no. 4 (1967), bibliography for 1962–65, 270 items.

257. Bulletin hispanique. (Universités de Bordeaux, de Toulouse, et de Poitiers.) Bordeaux. 1899– . Semiannual.
Also entitled **Annales de la Faculté des lettres de Bordeaux.**

Each volume normally contains several bibliographic sections which together report recent publications in Europe and the western hemisphere concerning Spanish literature, history, and linguistics. A bibliography of articles, divided into *Littérature, Histoire — civilisation,* and *Linguistique,* appears in the second number of each annual volume, along with a review of reviews containing signed summaries of significant articles in the major journals of the field, arranged by journal title. These two sections are complemented by critical reviews and short notices of current monographic publication which appear in each issue. Bibliography of articles began in 1957.
Examined: vol. 66 (1964), bibliography for 1963–64, *ca.* 250 items (bibliography of articles only).

258. Les dialectes belgo-romans. (Les amis de nos dialectes. Centre interuniversitaire de dialectologie wallonne.) Bruxelles, 1937– . Quarterly.

Beginning in 1952, this journal has published the same bibliography as **Handelingen van de Koninklijke Commissie voor Toponymie & Dialectologie. Bulletin de la Commission royale de toponymie & dialectologie (259).**

259. Handelingen van de Koninklijke Commissie voor Toponymie & Dialectologie. Bulletin de la Commission royale de toponymie & dialectologie. (Koninklijke Commissie voor Toponymie & Dialectologie.) Bruxelles. 1927– . Annual.

Each annual volume contains "La philologie wallonne," a bibliography of articles and books published during the previous year,

principally in Europe, concerning the philology of the Walloon dialects of Belgium up to the present. The publications are classified by topic, e.g. *Textes anciens; Littérature dialectale; Folklore, ethnographie; Toponymie.* Descriptive or critical annotations (up to 1,250 words). Book reviews are listed by author being reviewed. Author index; author indexes to vols. 1–25 of the **Handelingen** (publ. 1956) include an author index to this bibliography. Since 1952, this bibliography has also appeared in **Les dialectes belgo-romans (258).** This journal also publishes "De Nederlandse Taalkunde," "De Plaatsnamenstudie," and "De Persoonsnamenstudie" **(245).**
Examined: vol. 38 (1964), bibliography for 1963, 223 items.

*260. Nueva revista de filología hispánica. (Centro de estudios lingüísticos y literarios, Colegio de México. Facultad de humanidades, Universidad central de Venezuela.) México, D.F., and Caracas. 1947– . Semiannual.
Continues **Revista de filología hispánica.** (Instituto de filología, Universidad de Buenos Aires. Hispanic Institute, Columbia University.) Buenos Aires and New York. 1939–46.

Each issue contains an extensive bibliography of articles and books recently published in Europe and North and South America concerning philology, particularly of the romance languages. The publications are classified by topic under four major headings: *Sección general, Lingüística, Literatura, Folklore.* Occasional brief descriptive annotations. Reviews are noted. This journal also contains a section of book reviews and a section in which recent issues of important linguistic journals are surveyed. The bibliography began in 1939.
Examined: vol. 17 (1963–64), bibliography for 1961–63, 7,106 items.

261. La rassegna della letteratura italiana. Firenze. 1893– . Three issues yearly.

Each number contains a bibliography of articles and books recently published in Europe and North America concerning Italian literature from its origins, focusing on the twelfth century to the present. Publications are classified by century with a separate section for Dante. Descriptive or critical annotations

(up to 2,000 words). Book reviews are listed by reviewer. The bibliography assumed its present form in 1953.
Examined: vol. 68 (1964), bibliography for 1963, *ca.* 500 items.

262. Revista de filología española. (Instituto Miguel de Cervantes.) Madrid. 1914– . Semiannual.

Each issue contains a bibliography of articles and books recently published in Europe and the western hemisphere concerning the philology of the past and present languages of the Iberian peninsula. The publications are classified by topic in two major sections, *Lengua* and *Literatura*. Occasional brief descriptive annotations. Book reviews are noted. The journal also contains reviews of current books and a critical analysis of the contents of recent linguistic periodicals.
Examined: vol. 46 (1963, publ. 1965), bibliography for 1960–63, 1,615 items.

263. Revista portuguesa de filologia. (Instituto de estudos românicos, Universidade de Coimbra.) Coimbra. 1947– . Annual.

Each issue contains a bibliography of articles and books recently published in Europe and the western hemisphere concerning primarily romance philology and linguistics. The bibliography is arranged according to individual romance language, with additional sections devoted to such subjects as Greek and Latin, non-romance languages, and literature. Frequent descriptive annotations (up to 150 words). Reviews are noted. Author index.
Examined: vol. 13 (1964–65), bibliography for 1963–64, *ca.* 1,500 items.

*264. Romanische Bibliographie. Bibliographie romane. Romance Bibliography. K. Reichenberger, ed. Tübingen. 1961– (publ. 1965–). Irregular.
Supplement to **Zeitschrift für romanische Philologie.** Tübingen.
Continues **Zeitschrift für romanische Philologie: Supplement.** Tübingen. 1875–1960 (publ. 1877–1964).

A comprehensive bibliography of articles and books published during a given period, principally in Europe and the western hemisphere, concerning romance language and literature. The bibliography is classified into three major sections: I. *General Problems (Bibliographies; Periodicals; Serial Publications; Congresses, Research Institutes; Homage Volumes, Scholars' Biographies)*; II. *Linguistics (General Linguistics; Indo-European Linguistics; Substratum Languages; Latin; Superstratum Languages; Romance Linguistics: General; Rumanian; Istrian, Dalmatian, Albanian; Italian; Sardinian; Romansh; French; Provençal; Catalan; Spanish; Portuguese)*; III. *Literary History (General and Comparative Literary History; Latin Literature; Romance Literature; Rumanian Literature; Italian Literature; Sardinian Literature; Romansh Literature; French Literature; Provençal Literature; Catalan Literature; Spanish Literature; Portuguese Literature)*. Reviews are noted. Author and subject index.

Examined: vol. 1 (1961–62, publ. 1965–68), bibliography for 1961–62, 36,011 items, *ca.* 1,200 serials indexed.

265. Studi danteschi. (Società dantesca italiana.) Firenze. 1920–   . Annual.

This journal frequently contains a brief annotated list of articles and books published during a given year or years, primarily in Italy, concerning the life and writings of Dante. The publications are classified by general or biographic topic and by relevant work of Dante. Initialed descriptive annotations (up to 750 words).

Examined: vol. 41 (1964), bibliographies for 1959–63, 79 items.

266. Studi francesi. (Istituto di lingua e letteratura francese, Università di Torino.) Torino. 1957–   . Three issues yearly.

Each number contains a select bibliography of articles and books recently published in Europe and North America concerning French literature from the Middle Ages to the present. The publications are classified by historical period. Each item is accompanied by a descriptive or critical annotation of up to 2,000 words. Each issue also contains a limited number of signed critical reviews.

Examined: nos. 25–27 (1965), bibliography for 1963–64, *ca.* 1,000 items.

E. Slavic Languages

267. Polska Bibliografia literacka. (Instytut Badań Literackich, Polska Akademia Nauk.) Warszawa. 1944– (publ. 1957–). Biennial.

Each volume comprises an extensive bibliography of articles and books published during a given period, principally in Poland, concerning literature and literary criticism. The publications are classified by subject and by national literature. Reviews are noted. Subject and author indexes.

Examined: 1962–63 (publ. 1966), bibliography for 1962–63, 9,306 items, *ca.* 500 serials indexed.

268. Rocznik slawistyczny. Revue slavistique. (Komitety Językoznawstwa i Słowianoznawstwa.) Wrocław, Warszawa, Kraków. 1908– . Irregular.

The second issue of each volume normally comprises an extensive bibliography of articles and books published during a given year, primarily in Eastern Europe, concerning Slavic philology and literature. Classified by topic and Slavic language. Occasional descriptive annotations (up to 75 words). Reviews are noted. Author index.

Examined: vol. 23 (1964), bibliography for 1958, 2,535 items, *ca.* 200 serials indexed.

X. Music

*269. Bibliographie des Musikschrifttums. (Staatliches Institut für Musikforschung, Stiftung preussischer Kulturbesitz.) Frankfurt am Main. 1936– . Biennial.
Published 1936–38 as a supplement to **Archiv für Musikforschung.** (Staatliches Institut für deutsche Musikforschung.) Leipzig. And **Deutsche Musikkultur:** Zweimonatshefte für Musikleben und Musikforschung. (Staatliches Institut für Musikforschung zu Berlin.) Kassel.

Each volume comprises an extensive bibliography of articles and books published during a given two-year period, principally in Europe and North America, concerning the history and theory of Western music from its origins to the present. The publications are classified by topic and historical period within eight major sections: *Nachschlagewerke, Bibliotheken, Bibliographisches; Musikwissenschaft; Ethnologie und Anthropologie; Grundlagenforschung; Geschichte; Gegenwart; Instrumente; Einzelne Persönlichkeiten.* Indexes of authors and places and of names. Bibliography was not published for the years 1938–49.

Examined: 1958–59 (publ. 1964), bibliography for 1958–59, 7,915 items.

*270. Musica disciplina: A Yearbook of the History of Music. (American Institute of Musicology.) Roma. 1946– . Annual.

Each volume normally contains a bibliography of articles and books published during the previous year in Europe and North America concerning religious and secular music, with emphasis on the medieval and renaissance period. The publications are listed alphabetically by author in four sections: *Books, Articles, Dissertations,* and *Music* (i.e. scores).

Examined: vol. 20 (1966), bibliography for 1965, *ca.* 250 items.

271. Revue de musicologie. (Société française de musicologie.) Paris. 1917– . Semiannual.

The second issue of each annual volume contains a list of select tables of contents of journals devoted to musicology and other journals which contain material on musicology. An effort is made to include all relevant articles published in France and in major non-French journals. The tables of contents are arranged by country of publication. Each issue of this journal also contains critical reviews of current books and music scores.

Examined: vol. 51 (1965), bibliography for 1964–65, 81 journals, 17 reviews.

Addendum:

RILM Abstracts: Répertoire international de la littérature musicale. International Repertory of Music Literature. Internationales Repertorium der Musikliteratur. (International RILM Center, Queens College, City University of New York.) Flushing. 1967– (publ. 1968–). Quarterly.

See also:

140. **Répertoire général de sciences religieuses**
141. **Revue d'histoire ecclésiastique: Bibliographie**
145. **Ostkirchliche Studien**
   Section VIII-B, Liturgy and Hagiography

XI. Science, Technology, and Medicine

272. Bibliography of the History of Medicine. (National Library of Medicine.) Bethesda, Maryland. 1965–   (publ. 1966–   ). Annual.

An extensive bibliography of articles and books published throughout the world during a given year concerning all aspects of the history of medicine from the earliest times through the modern era. The majority of the entries are supplied by the National Library of Medicine's MEDLARS, which indexes some 2,500 serial titles. The bibliography is divided into three parts: The first, *Biographies and Famous Persons,* contains publications relating to physicians and other individuals. The second, *Subject Index,* includes all aspects of medical history, and is extensively subdivided by topic and historical period. Certain titles appear in both parts I and II. The third part, *Authors,* lists the publications appearing in parts I and II alphabetically by author. Quinquennial cumulations are planned.

Examined: vol. 1 (1965, publ. 1966), bibliography for 1964–65, *ca.* 2,500 items, *ca.* 2,500 serials indexed.

273. Bulletin de liaison du Centre international d'étude des textiles anciens. (Centre international d'étude des textiles anciens.) Lyon. 1955– . Semiannual.

Each number contains a bibliography of articles and books recently published throughout the world concerning the study of textiles as an aspect of the history of art and technology. Classified by topic, e.g. *Costumes, Histoire et commerce, Tapisseries.* Descriptive annotations (up to 100 words).
   Examined: nos. 21–22 (1965), bibliography for 1963–65, *ca.* 400 items.

274. Bulletin signalétique 22: Histoire des sciences et des techniques. (Centre national de la recherche scientifique.) Paris. 1947– . Quarterly.

An extensive bibliography of articles recently published throughout the world concerning the history of science and technology. The publications are classified by topic within six major sections: general (including the relationship of science and religion), mathematics, physics (including cosmology and astronomy), technology (including transportation, paper, weaponry), earth sciences (including mining and agriculture), and life sciences (including medicine and hospitals). Descriptive annotations (up to 150 words). This bibliography appears as a separate publication and also as section 22 of the **Bulletin signalétique (5).** Annual author and subject indexes.
   Examined: vol. 20 (1966), bibliography for 1964–65, 4,443 items, *ca.* 2,500 serials indexed (for sections 19–24 of the **Bulletin**).

*275. Current Work in the History of Medicine: An International Bibliography. (Wellcome Historical Medical Library.) London. 1954– . Quarterly.

Each number comprises a bibliography of articles recently published throughout the world concerning the history of medicine (with emphasis on western Europe) from antiquity to the present. Titles are listed within an extensive subject classification in dictionary form and are accompanied by a list of authors' addresses and an author index. A list of new books or books to be published on the history of medicine is also included.

Examined: nos. 45–48 (1965), bibliography for 1964–65, 5,202 articles, *ca.* 750 books.

276. Index zur Geschichte der Medizin, Naturwissenschaft und Technik. (Deutsche Vereinigung für Geschichte der Medizin, Naturwissenschaft und Technik.) München and Berlin. 1953– . Irregular.

Each issue contains two bibliographies, "Medizinhistorische Bibliographie" and "Naturwissenschaften Bibliographie," which include articles and books published during a given period, primarily in Europe and North America, concerning all aspects of the history of medicine, science, and technology. Publications in the first bibliography are classified by topic or chronological period under three major headings: *Geschichte der Medizin, Geschichte der Zahnheilkunde, Geschichte der Pharmazie.* Publications in the second bibliography are classified by topic under two major headings: *Geschichte der exakten Wissenschaften und Technik* and *Geschichte der Biologie.*
Examined: vol. 2 (1966), bibliography for 1949–52, 7,129 items.

*277. Isis: An International Review Devoted to the History of Science and Its Cultural Influences. (History of Science Society. Smithsonian Institution.) Washington, D.C. 1913– . Quarterly.

One number of each annual volume normally contains the "Critical Bibliography of the History of Science and Its Cultural Influences," an extensive bibliography of articles and books published throughout the world during the previous year concerning "the history of science and its cultural influences." The publications are classified within four sections: *History of Sciences: General References & Tools, Science & Its History from Special Points of View, Histories of the Special Sciences, Chronological Classifications.* Each is extensively subdivided into specific topics, historical periods, geographic areas, and scientific disciplines. Frequent signed descriptive annotations (up to 250 words). Reviews are noted. Index of names (excluding reviewers).
Examined: vol. 56 (1965), bibliography for 1963–64, *ca.* 2,000 items, *ca.* 500 serials indexed.

134   SERIAL BIBLIOGRAPHIES

278. Journal of Glass Studies. (Corning Museum of Glass, Corning Glass Center.) Corning, New York. 1959– . Annual.

Each volume contains a bibliography of articles and books published during the previous year, primarily in Europe and North America, concerning both the technological and the artistic aspects of the history of glass from antiquity to the present. Classified by topic, historical period, and geographic area. Book reviews are listed by reviewer. Occasional brief descriptive annotations.
Examined: vol. 8 (1966), bibliography for 1965, *ca.* 525 items.

279. The Journal of the Arms and Armour Society. (Arms and Armour Society.) London. 1953– . Quarterly.

Each number normally contains a brief bibliography of articles and books recently published in Europe and North America concerning arms and armor and their history, from antiquity through the nineteenth century. Publications are classified within three sections: *Recent Publications; Museum and Exhibition Catalogues, Handbooks, etc.;* and *Periodicals Devoted Entirely to Arms and Armour* (tables of contents of relevant journals). Occasional brief descriptive annotations.
Examined: vol. 4 (1962–64), bibliography for 1961–64, *ca.* 250 items.

280. The Journal of Transport History. Leicester. 1953– Semiannual.

The first and third numbers of each biennial volume contain a bibliography of articles and government documents published in Britain during the previous year concerning primarily land transport and harbors in the British Isles from prehistoric times through the present. Publications are listed by serial title. Government publications are listed in a separate section.
Examined: vol. 6 (1963–64), bibliographies for 1962 and 1963, 96 items.

281. Lychnos: Lärdomshistoriska samfundets årsbok. Annual of the Swedish History of Science Society. Stockholm, Göteborg, and Uppsala. 1936– . Biennial.

Each volume normally contains a bibliography of articles and books published in Sweden during the previous year concerning Western intellectual history, in particular the history of science, or published in Europe and North America concerning the history of science in Sweden. Classified by topic, including the history of theology, law, medicine, natural science, and technology. Reviews are noted. Occasional brief descriptive annotations.

Examined: 1963–64 (publ. 1965), bibliography for 1962, *ca.* 500 items.

282. Scientiarum historia: Driemaandelijks Tijdschrift voor de Geschiedenis van de Geneeskunde, Wiskunde en Natuurwetenschappen. Antwerpen. 1959– . Quarterly.

One or more issues of each annual volume normally contain a bibliography of articles and books recently published throughout the world concerning the history of science and technology in the Low Countries (Benelux) up to the present. Classified by topic. Occasional brief descriptive annotations. The bibliography was devoted to the Netherlands only until 1966.

Examined: vol. 8 (1966), bibliography for 1964–65, *ca.* 150 items.

283. Technology and Culture. (Society for the History of Technology.) Chicago. 1959– . Quarterly.

The second issue of each annual volume contains "Current Bibliography in the History of Technology," which includes articles and books published throughout the world during a given year concerning the "development of technology and its relations with society and culture." The bibliography is classified by topic: *General and Collected Works; Documentation; Biography; Technical Societies, Technical Education; Economic, Business, Political, and Social History, Travels and Description; General Relationships between Technology and Culture; Civil Engineering; Transportation; Energy Conversion; Material and Processes; Mechanical and Electro-Mechanical Technology; Communication and Records; Agricultural and Food Technology; Industrial Organization; Military Technology.* Descriptive annotations (up to 75 words). Reviews are occasionally noted. Author and subject indexes. Vol. 8 contains subject indexes for the first four issues of the bibliography. The bibliography began in 1964 (for 1962.)

Examined: vol. 8 (1967), bibliography for 1965, *ca.* 425 items.

Addenda:

Journal of the History of Behavioral Sciences. Brandon. 1965– . Quarterly.

Mitteilungen zur Geschichte der Medizin und der Naturwissenschaften. (Deutsche Akademie der Naturforscher Leopoldina. Deutsche Gesellschaft für Geschichte der Medizin, Naturwissenschaft und Technik.) Leipzig. 1902–42, 1961– . Irregular.

See also:

24. **Revue bibliographique de sinologie**
120. **Artes textiles**
141. **Revue d'histoire ecclésiastique: Bibliographie**

Index of Titles

[Numerals refer to item numbers in this bibliography; those in boldface indicate a main entry]

Antiquaries Journal, **116**
Anzeiger für schweizerische Geschichte, **50**
Apollinaris: Commentarius iuris canonici, **175**
Árbók (Landsbokasafn Íslands), **72**
Archaeological Bibliography for Great Britain & Ireland, **117**
Archäologische Bibliographie, **118**
Archäologischer Anzeiger, 118
Archief voor de Geschiedenis van de Katholieke Kerk in Nederland, **156**
Archiv für katholisches Kirchenrecht, **176**
Archiv für Liturgiewissenschaft, **200**
Archiv für Musikforschung, 269
Archivalische Zeitschrift, **103**
Der Archivar: Mitteilungsblatt für deutsches Archivwesen, **104**
Archives de sociologie des religions, **137**
Archivum: Revue internationale des archives, 106
Archivum bibliographicum carmelitanum, **148**
Archivum historiae pontificiae, **157**
Arte veneta: Rivista di storia dell'arte, **119**
Artes textiles: Bijdragen tot de Geschiedenis van de Tapijt-, Borduur- en Textielkunst, **120**
Arts et traditions populaires, **187**
Atti della Società ligure di storia patria, **69**
Augustiniana: Tijdschrift voor de Studie van Sint Augustinus en de Augustijnenorde, **149, 207**
Ausgrabungen und Funde: Nachrichtenblatt für Vor- und Frühgeschichte, **121**
Auswahlbibliographie zur Geschichte und Landeskunde der Sudetenländer, **88**

Baltische Bibliographie, **38**
Bayerische Bibliographie, **49**
Bayerische Vorgeschichtsblätter, **122**
Beitrǽge zur romanischen Philologie, **254**
Belgisch Tijdschrift voor Filologie en Geschiedenis, **31**
Biblica: Commentarii ad rem biblicam scientifice investigandam, 194
Bibliografi til norges historie, **73**
Bibliografia armena, **146**
Bibliografia copta, **146**
Bibliografía de Galicia, **89**
Bibliografia dell'antichità cristiana, **134**
Bibliografia dell'Archivio Vaticano, **105**
Bibliografia filosofica italiana, **208**
Bibliografia filosofica italiana dal 1900 al 1950, 208
Bibliografia greca, **146**
Bibliografia historii polskiej, **78**
Bibliografia italiana di storia del diritto medievale e moderno, **173**
Bibliografia metodica degli studi di egittologia e di papirologia, **143**
Bibliografia periodica sistematica internazionale di storia amministrativa, **172**
Bibliografia romana, **70**

French Historical Studies, **47**

General and Historical Studies, **240**
Geographical Abstracts, **170**
Germania: Anzeiger der Römisch-germanischen Kommission des Deutschen archäologischen Instituts, **128**
Germanistik: Internationales Referatenorgan mit bibliographischen Hinweisen, **244**
Geschichte in Wissenschaft und Unterricht, **56**
Geschichtliche und landeskundliche Literatur Pommerns, **88**
Gnomon: Kritische Zeitschrift für die gesamte klassische Altertumswissenschaft, **252**

Hamburger Beiträge zur Numismatik, **111**
Handelingen van de Koninklijke Commissie voor Toponymie & Dialectologie, **245**, **258**, **259**
Handelingen van het Genootschap voor Geschiedenis Gesticht onder de Benaming Société d'émulation te Brugge, **29**
Hansische Geschichtsblätter, **163**
Hansische Umschau, **163**
Helinium: Revue consacrée à l'archéologie des Pays-Bas, de la Belgique et du Grand Duché de Luxembourg, **129**
Historia agriculturae, **164**
Historia rerum rusticarum, 161
Historisk tidskrift, **75**
Historisk tidsskrift, **73**

Imago mundi: A Review of Early Cartography, **171**
Index bibliographicus Gandensis, **206**
Index Islamicus: A Catalogue of Articles on Islamic Subjects in Periodicals and Other Collective Publications, **98**
Index to Foreign Legal Periodicals, **179**
Index to Legal Periodicals, **180**
Index translationum: Répertoire international des traductions, **9**
Index zur Geschichte der Medizin, Naturwissenschaft und Technik, **276**
Índice histórico español, **90**
International Bibliography of Economics, **165**
International Bibliography of Historical Sciences, **10**
International Bibliography of Political Science, **181**
International Bibliography of Social and Cultural Anthropology, **189**
International Bibliography of Sociology, **190**
International Bibliography of the History of Religions, **139**
International Bibliography of the Social Sciences, 165, 181, 189, 190
International Folklore Bibliography, **191**
International Guide to Medieval Studies: A Quarterly Index to Periodical Literature, **11**
International Medieval Bibliography, **12**
International Review of Biblical Studies, **196**
Internationale Bibliographie der Geschichtswissenschaften, **10**
Internationale volkskundliche Bibliographie, **191**

Index of Editors*

*See above, p. xii n. 15.